THE ACCIDENTAL BUDDHIST

ALSO BY DINTY W. MOORE

The Emperor's Virtual Clothes

THE
ACCIDENTAL
BUDDHIST

Mindfulness, Enlightenment,

and Sitting Still

DINTY W. MOORE

Algonquin Books of Chapel Hill   1997

Published by
ALGONQUIN BOOKS OF CHAPEL HILL
Post Office Box 2225
Chapel Hill, North Carolina 27515-2225

a division of
WORKMAN PUBLISHING
708 Broadway
New York, New York 10003

"The Ballad of the Skeleton," from *Selected Poems 1947–1995*, by Allen
Ginsberg. Harper Collins, 1996. Reprinted by permission of the author.

Library of Congress Cataloging-in-Publication Data
Moore, Dinty W., 1955–
    The accidental Buddhist : mindfulness, enlightenment, and sitting
still / Dinty W. Moore.
        p. cm.
    Includes bibliographical references.
    ISBN 1-56512-142-2 (hardcover)
    1. Spiritual life—Buddhism. 2. Moore, Dinty W., 1955–
3. Buddhism—United States. I. Title.
BQ5405.M656 1997
294.3'0973—DC21   97-19918
                                                                    CIP

10 9 8 7 6 5 4 3 2 1
First Edition

TO MARIA RAPHAELLA ROMASCO MOORE

TEACHER, DAUGHTER, AND FRIEND

ACKNOWLEDGMENTS

MY DEEP THANKS to the many Buddhist practitioners who offered assistance during the course of this project, including Linsi Deyo and Patrick Clark, Dharman Craig Presson, Mary Pattison, Bill Butler and Jean Giddings, Barbara and Len Seibert, Steve Heywood, Lynn Newman Mennenga, Tom and Sue Wolsko, and Jack Hatfield. And *gassho* to my patient teachers: John Daido Loori, Geshe Lobsang Tenzin Negi, Father Robert J. Kennedy, Bhante Henepola Gunaratana, and Dai-En Bennage. I am grateful as well to Helen Tworkov for her kindness, and to Allen Ginsberg for permission to use an excerpt of his poem "The Ballad of the Skeletons."

During the time I worked on this book, I received significant support from the Institute for Arts and Humanistic Studies at Pennsylvania State University, from Kjell Meling, and from the Penn State Altoona Campus Advisory Board.

A special thanks to Robert Rubin for all he has taught me. May his own journey go well.

And finally, for her patience, guidance, and love, a deep bow of gratitude to Renita Romasco.

There is something in other people's religions that is incomprehensible.

—Huston Smith

I'm astounded by people who want to "know" the universe when it's hard enough to find your way around Chinatown.

—Woody Allen

CONTENTS

THE ACCIDENTAL BUDDHIST

PRELUDE

....

WHEN I WAS young, I thought for a while that I might actually become a priest. I was raised in a town full of Catholics and endured twelve years of Catholic school, so the idea was certainly bouncing around. The priesthood, after all, is the ultimate calling, every Irish-American mother's dream for her son. I had a few nuns in my family, a priest related by marriage, and I was painfully awkward around girls, so why not?

It turned out, of course, that I didn't have a true calling, or any calling, but there were moments when I thought I might. Most prominent among them was a weekend in early high school. I was barely fifteen, searching for something about myself more interesting than being the school's best speller, and so agreed not only to participate in a Catholic Youth retreat weekend, but to lure ten or so of my classmates to come along.

I was attending an all-male Catholic prep school in my hometown, and the main selling point for the retreat was that we would be joined by an equal number of saintly young girls from Mercyhurst and Villa Maria. Three days and two nights in a monastery, along the scenic shores of Lake Erie, with only a few doddering monks as chaperones. Anything could happen.

But none of it did. They watched us like hawks, and there were so many locked doors and thick walls between the girls' dorm and the boys' dorm that it would have required heavy machinery to break through. It was late November, and the idea of sneaking down to the lakeshore for some heavy petting was discouraged well enough by thirty-mile-per-hour subzero Canadian winds.

Instead, we were left to think and pray. The first night, we sat against the walls of a darkened first-floor hallway, listening to the Moody Blues on a record player. This was the age of guitar masses, and the monks were trying hard to be relevant, I suppose. We were supposed to be thinking about Jesus, how he had died for our sins and could save us again from our adolescent weakness, but I was thinking about Mary Margaret Flatley.

Mary Margaret was the Catholic Youth recruiter for Mercyhurst Girl's High School. She was beautiful. I imagined that if she saw how devout I was, she would want to lose her virginity to me.

I prayed fervently all weekend, and when it came time to tell the assembled group about what was in our minds, I tried hard to sound deep and soulful. "There is so much good inside of people," I whispered. "If only we just loved one another."

Any number of young Catholic girls decided over those three days that I was a great guy, very sincere, and sweet. Not one of them, of course, had any interest in dating me. I was stuck talking to Brother Damien.

Brother Damien was the youngest of the monks, probably in his thirties, and he somehow knew that my parents were divorced, that my father had a drinking problem going back twenty years, and that

I was bright, eager, and fit in nowhere. Maybe everybody is massively insecure at age fifteen, but I wore my insecurity on my sleeve. He took me aside late Saturday afternoon.

"I've been noticing you," he said, out of earshot of the others. "They call you Dinty, but your name should be Peter, like the Apostle, because you are a rock. Do you know that?"

I think I nodded.

"You are very strong. I can sense it. There is a rock inside of you."

I nodded again. I had noticed the rock. I thought it was everything wrong about me, all my faults and deficiencies balled up and ready to explode, but Brother Damien made it sound like something good.

"That rock is your faith," he went on. "That rock is the faith that keeps you strong. You are going to do great things."

The monk took my breath away. He looked right at me, not averting his gaze, not nervously shuffling off. He just looked at me and waited. No priest or monk had ever paid such attention to me before. I don't think *any* adult had ever paid such attention to me. Brother Damien was a man of God, so in a sense, it was God paying attention to me.

We were just off the chapel, and I could hear the other monks reciting their Latin prayers. It was the most religious moment of my life.

IT TURNS OUT, though, that the rock was something else entirely. Mary Margaret Flatley took up with a lifeguard, my divorced mother married a fellow I never really trusted or liked, my high school religion teacher flunked me for asking hard questions, and my father fell off the wagon. I would walk home from school some days and see his old car bouncing off the curbs and boulevards as he threaded his way from the Danish Club to Mentley's Tavern. That hard thing inside of me turned out to be anger.

My life was a mess, a mess not even of my own making. And the situation didn't get any better, either, after God, through Brother Damien, took a direct interest in me. It just got worse.

I began to suspect that when the old priests and nuns who had been guiding me through my childhood and early adolescence said "we must take the truth of Jesus on faith," what they were really saying was "we have absolutely no proof of any of this, so you are pretty much on your own." Being a good kid and saying my prayers wasn't going to fix anything.

I never went back to Brother Damien's monastery, and it wasn't long before I stopped going to church at all. Stopped praying. Stopped looking for spiritual answers. God, I thought, had let me down.

NONE OF WHICH fully explains why twenty-five years later I found myself at the doorway of a different monastery. This one, as it happens, was also in New York State, but far on the opposite end. And the monks, well, this time the monks were Buddhists.

My journey, it turned out, was not quite finished.

PART 1

ZEN MIND, MUDDLED MIND

1

BUDDHA 101

Stumbling Up Monkey Mind Mountain

ZEN MOUNTAIN MONASTERY is an impressive stone structure tucked neatly onto the side of Tremper Mountain, in the Catskills, in eastern New York State.

I arrive there with a fair degree of trepidation on a Friday evening and am directed to a second-floor dorm room. There are eight bunk beds and a sink crammed into the small area. When I stumble in, Harold, a sixty-something attorney with a neatly trimmed white beard, has already marked out his territory by spreading his expensive luggage in a wide circle.

He introduces himself amicably enough, but only as an excuse, it seems, to make it clear to me within seconds that he knows more about Zen, Buddhism, and meditation than anyone, other than perhaps the Buddha himself. He mentions the many *zendos* where he has studied, the Zen *koans* (riddles, more or less) he has contemplated, the teachers he has spoken with, and throws around an impressive array of foreign-sounding words.

I am stuck listening to the boasting because Harold has blocked my way to where I hope to make my bunk, and because Wayne, the only other roommate to have arrived at this point, has wisely retreated to his bed, where he quietly reads a book.

It takes some work, but I manage to extricate myself from Harold's lecture and find a corner bed. From there, all I have to do is watch the room fill up and wonder what the heck I am doing in a monastery anyway. It has been ages since Brother Damien took me aside, and it feels odd to be back.

SOMETIME AFTER DARK, I join a handful of other spiritual greenhorns for dinner, a tasty assortment of vegetables, spiced and stir-fried, served over rice. We are next herded into the Buddha Hall, a small room with no chairs, no tables, no real furniture, just an altar topped with framed photos of old Asian men, probably deceased Buddhist teachers, and lots of round black pillows scattered across the carpet.

There is discernible anxiety in the room, though we have all come willingly—in fact, we have paid for the privilege. Many in attendance have come from New York City, just a few hours to the east. Other have come across state from Ithaca, Albany, or Rochester. I have driven six hours from Central Pennsylvania.

We range in age from early twenties to mid-sixties, and except for our loose cotton clothing, it strikes me that we would not look much different if we had come for a business seminar, or a weekend of bird-watching.

With our shoes left out in the hall, we sit on the thin carpet and nervously check out one another's socks, lost in our individual fears. How long, I wonder, can I sit in silent meditation without going totally nuts?

At the front of the room, a Japanese woman settles onto a pillow, carefully arranges the hems of her flowing black robes, then slowly tucks the hems under her knees. She is quite compact, barely more than four feet tall, but sturdily built. Her head is shaved.

"My name is Jimon," she says, in a soft, pleasant voice. There is no trace of an accent, so she probably isn't Japanese after all. She is probably Japanese-American. It doesn't matter, of course, except that I am full of curiosity. Buddhism is an Asian religion, the monastery is run for American students, and I'm already wondering where the two cultures are going to gently intersect and where they are going to slam right into one another.

"I'm here to introduce you to Zen practice," the woman continues. "The most important part of that practice is sitting, and there are a few good ways to do this."

She tells us that the round pillows on the floor are called *zafus*, and describes the various ways they can be used for support, then outlines the different postures—full lotus, half lotus, and kneeling. For those of us who can't handle the pillows, she points to small, individual wooden benches—you sit on the slanted bench, and tuck your legs underneath, so there is less pressure on the knees. She calls them *seiza* benches.

"And for anyone who can't handle that," Jimon says, smiling, "you can sit on a chair."

The weekend newcomers breathe a collective sigh of relief. Jimon's voice, her very manner in fact, is reassuring, and now that she has promised us that we won't be forced to dislocate our knees, we are feeling pretty good. *Gee,* I can almost hear a few people behind me thinking, *who said this was going to be hard?*

"More important than how you sit is what you do with your mind," she informs us, and that turns out to be the difficult part.

During meditation, the mind is supposed to be still. But the mind doesn't want to be still. In fact, left to its own devices, the mind would prefer to babble, jabber, and prattle all day—rushing from thought to thought, worry to worry, and generally keeping us as far away from enlightenment as possible. Buddhists call this Monkey Mind, Jimon says. The path of human thinking can be thought of as being like a monkey in the jungle, constantly swinging from vine to vine, tree to tree, seldom lighting for more than a second before it is off again.

She suggests we count our breaths as a way to combat the mental anarchy. If you focus on the count, she promises, it will distract you from the inner dialogue. And if that doesn't work, she adds, there is always the stick.

"During the long periods of sitting tomorrow, if you feel that your shoulders are too tight, someone will come along with a stick, and you can request that they hit your accupressure points," she explains softly. "You make this request by bringing the hands together in the prayer position and bowing."

The anxiety in the room instantly resurfaces. Someone behind me whispers "Ouch" at the thought of being smacked with a long piece of lumber. A small, nervous laugh ripples from pillow to pillow. We have probably all read stories along the way about Zen masters who punch their students in the nose, cut off their ears, or somehow do them bodily harm because they lack diligence.

Jimon, though, just smiles her reassuring smile.

"Oh, it doesn't hurt," she promises. "The *kyosaku* stick is made of soft wood."

We are released to our bedrooms with that thought on our minds. Tomorrow we will "sit *zazen*"—meditate—in earnest, so for now, we all need a good night's sleep.

SATURDAY

Thanks to Harold, though, I barely sleep at all.

He is tucked into a Polartek sleeping bag barely two feet from my metal bunk, and all through the long chilly night, he chants "Za-aaaazzzzzeeeeeeen . . . zaaaazzzzzeeeeen."

The snoring is insistent, steady, as if the glottal vibrations were his secret mantra. If I was any sort of Buddhist at all, I probably would not have spent the wee hours entertaining so many murderous thoughts about the man, but I'm not any sort of Buddhist, and I want to choke him.

At precisely five A.M., a sudden bell clangs along the darkened hallways. Wayne fights himself free of his covers first, then shakes the still-snoring Harold by the shoulders. Wake-up time.

We have been told to maintain full silence until after the dawn meditation session, and everyone in my room complies. There is no time for small talk anyway. No time even for a morning shower. Like zazen zombies, we pull on our cold, wrinkled clothes and spill out into the monastery's massive meditation hall.

Then we sit.

In a big open room, on squat black pillows, with incense swirling past our noses and all manner of cluttered thoughts jumping through our unaccustomed brains, we sit.

And sit some more.

THE SITTING PART does not turn out to be particularly difficult. So early in the morning, my bones are more than happy to hold perfectly still. My brain though, is another story.

Jimon warned us about Monkey Mind, and she was right on the money. My inner dialogue erupts almost before my bottom hits the zafu: *Oh, I am doing meditation, how relaxing, oops, I shouldn't be think-*

ing so much, my knee hurts, wait, just focus on the breath, is that a woman in front of me or a guy with long hair, pretty hair anyway, wonder what's for lunch, hey, wait, count your breath, one, two, three, four, did I turn off my car lights?

Jimon not only warned us that our minds might do this, she also warned us that we would find it discouraging. This racing mind stuff trips up many beginning meditators. They find that they can't quiet the stream of distraction, and so, discouraged, they give up on meditation altogether.

Stick with it, she advised.

So I persist, but the truth is, I turn out to have a particularly unrelenting monkey. He not only swings from tree to tree, he rips off big green leaves and chatters at the top of his monkey lungs, an angry baboon somehow set loose in an espresso bar.

Following Jimon's instructions, I try to bypass the monkey by counting my breaths. The first "in" breath is one, the second is two, the third is three, but my Monkey Mind is stubbornly uncooperative. More often than not, I lose track around five or seven. Needless to say, *nirvana* completely eludes me.

The sitting meditation ends eventually, and we all stand by our pillows. Pretty soon, a bell rings.

Along with the thirty or so of us newcomers, thirty or so others in long gray robes are seated further toward the middle of the monastery's large meditation hall. They are the advanced students, I assume. Most of those in gray robes don't have shaved heads, but a handful of more serious-seeming types in black robes, *with* shaved heads, sit in the front rows. I'm focusing on hairstyles here, because I am still trying to figure out who is a monk, who is not, and where it all fits together. None of this has been explained.

Suddenly, those in the know begin chanting in Japanese: *"No mo san man da moto nan oha ra chi koto sha sono nan to ji to en gya gya gya ki gya."*

I am handed a card with the words, so that I can chant, too, though I have no idea what the words mean, and no one attempts to explain. Off and on during the ensuing service, we bow from the waist, and then, following the gray robes in the row ahead of me, I learn the full prostration bow—falling to the knees and bowing on the floor.

At various points, assorted black robes and gray robes approach the main altar, then back away. Sometimes they carry incense boxes, other times they carry items I can't identify.

It begins to seem awfully familiar: the seemingly pointless walking back and forth, the retrieval of various objects only to put them right back where they started out, the chanting in a foreign tongue —it reminds me of morning mass at Good Shepherd Catholic Church when I was a boy. I never understood what was being said then either, not knowing Latin, and though I knew what the priests were up to in a vague sort of way—they were consecrating the bread and wine into the body and blood of Christ—they seemed to have found perhaps the most inefficient manner imaginable to accomplish this sacred task. The old priests reminded me of amnesiacs in a kitchen, always turning back to the cupboard to get something they forgot, putting things down in the wrong place, and then later having to cross the room to get those same things.

To say this about Catholic Mass is a sacrilege, and if I had expressed these thoughts in front of one of my grade school nuns, I surely would have felt a sharp rap, and not from the soft wood of the *kyosaku* stick, either.

I don't know enough about Buddhism yet to know if I'm being sacrilegious here, too, or, if so, what I'm supposed to do, or say, or think about it. Jimon has mentioned nothing about venial sin.

Eventually, though, I relax and begin to enjoy the Zen liturgy for what it is—rather interesting, exotic, and nonthreatening. No one is going to make me take communion. No one is going force me into the confessional. Sister Mary Catherine is not coming up behind me to pull my ear.

And anyway, the chants are invigorating, and we are able to move around finally—stand and bow, stand and bow twice, turn, stand and bow, deep bow—instead of just staring at a blank wall.

WHEN THE CEREMONY finally concludes—for no reason clear to me except that another bell rings and everyone stops—we are herded down narrow, winding steps to the monastery's massive dining hall. Our breakfast is steaming on long tables, but first the head cook lights incense at another small altar and leads us in yet another chant, this time in English:

> First, seventy-two labors brought us this food
> We should know how it comes to us
> Second, as we receive this offering
> We should consider
> Whether our virtue and practice deserve it

My virtue and practice have been pretty inconsequential to this point, but I'm hungry. The oatmeal is hot, and we are finally allowed to talk.

Five of us end up at one table, including Harold, my snoring roommate, complaining that, in fact, it was *he* who didn't get much sleep at all.

"Someone's watch was going off all night," he says, looking pointedly in my direction, raising a gray eyebrow. "Does anyone know whose watch that might have been?"

We all shrug.

"Kept me awake," Harold complains, shaking his head from side to side. "Damn thing beeped all through the night."

He looks around the table at each of us, again resting his eyes on me a bit longer than on the others. "Anybody know whose watch that was?"

I am truly and absolutely clueless. My watch did beep, as a matter of fact, once every hour, but not only was the sound nearly imperceptible, especially when hidden under a pillow and squashed by my large Irish head, but I know for a fact, since I was wearing the watch, and checking it on occasion, that old Harold was snoring from two-thirty to five A.M., uninterrupted snoring of the deepest and most annoying kind. He wouldn't have heard a bomb go off. He didn't even hear the loud bell that was supposed to awaken us before dawn.

Yet he heard my Timex?

It was my first Zen *koan*.

2

ONE BRIGHT IDEA

My American Buddhism Project

AFTER SEEKING THE tranquillity that comes through Buddhist meditation for roughly half a day or so, only one conclusion makes any sense: I have Attention Deficit Disorder. I am too scattered, too undisciplined, too easily distracted, to focus on anything.

True of me certainly, this is true as well of most of the people I know. One uniting characteristic of our times is that we skitter from thing to thing, eating while we talk, reading while we eat, chatting on the phone while we watch TV, thinking about work while we dress our kids for school, daydreaming about our weekend while we work. We put phones in our cars, install televisions in our bathrooms, pipe music into every shopping mall and public space, erect flashing signs along every roadway. We seem to be fleeing stillness as if it were some curse, yet ironically, many of us are starting to actively seek it out.

I am not the only one exploring Buddhism right now—there is, in fact, a modest surge underway. The interest that has been rooted for quite some time in cultural centers such as New York, Los Angeles, and San Francisco is starting to spread inward. *Zendos,* monasteries, and meditation centers are popping up in every state, in the cities, in the college towns, and even in rural corners such as Floyds Knobs, Indiana, and High View, West Virginia. Start paying attention, and you'll notice more and more references to Buddhism, Zen, and mindfulness on television, in the news, in the casual speech of those around you. Vice President Al Gore visited a California monastery just before the last election, though he may regret it now.

Hollywood is playing its part with a string of recent and upcoming movies, such as *Little Buddha, Seven Years in Tibet,* and *Kundun.* Richard Gere is a Buddhist, and makes it known. So are Tina Turner, Oliver Stone, and Chicago Bulls head coach Phil Jackson. Rocker/ actress Courtney Love took the ashes of her dead husband, Kurt Cobain, to India, to be embedded in a Buddhist shrine. Walk the streets of any medium to large city these days, and you will see faddish Buddha T-shirts, *om mani padme om* tattoos, and Tibetan folk-art boutiques.

While a good number of Americans are embracing serious religious Buddhist practice, many, many others are engaging in "vaguely" Buddhist practice, much of it part of the New Age movement. *Business Week* hails meditation as "the new balm for corporate stress." Even beat cops are being taught to breathe, for relaxation. Beermaker Adolph Coors reports that meditation has helped lower the company's mental health costs 27 percent since 1987.

And still other Americans are engaged in wildly shallow and seemingly absurd Buddhist practice. *Elle* magazine, of all places, ran a recent series of articles promoting the meditative lifestyle. In one article, Buddhist psychiatrist Mark Epstein endorses a group of New Yorkers who have begun chanting for parking spaces. "It definitely works," he offered. "I always get a parking place that way, just by asking for one."

Even Bart Simpson, the cartoon character, has taken up the subject, finally determining just exactly what "one hand clapping" sounds like. He may be our first animated Zen master.

Buddhism is a religion with a sense of humor, and I'm guessing the Buddha liked a good laugh as well. I don't know for sure what all this scattered interest in Buddhism means exactly, but I do know that our interest is growing.

Why?

Yankelovich Partners, Inc., the polling firm, occasionally asks Americans how many think that life has become too complicated. In 1985, just over half said "yes." At the end of 1996, that proportion had climbed to 73 percent. Many of us are beginning to realize that we need *some* tranquillity, or we are going to explode.

Perhaps our flirtation with Buddhism as the twenty-first century fast approaches is a cry for help from a chronically active culture. We are truly the Distracted Generation. It is hard to hear your own heartbeat when your pager is beeping, your car phone is ringing, and a stream of faxes is pouring out of your Danka.

Did someone say mindfulness?

Did someone suggest meditation?

Hell, we can hardly breathe.

AS FOR MYSELF, I had toyed with Buddhist philosophy in my young adulthood. Like millions of other college kids, I read Pirsig's *Zen and the Art of Motorcycle Maintenance* in one long weekend, put it down thinking my life had been forever transformed, then promptly forgot about it. I even took a meditation class once, but never got past how to fold my legs.

One day, many years later, though, I chanced upon a book called

Being Peace by a Vietnamese monk named Thich Nhat Hanh, and something was awakened in me. Not any deep faith in God, to be honest, but just enough curiosity to start me thinking again. What was it that these Buddhists had discovered? What was I missing?

Most striking to me about Nhat Hanh's book was the fact that the Zen monk didn't talk about man's shortcomings, our undeservedness, or the necessity of suffering. He talked about being happy. He talked about how if we were happy and kind, we would pass this happiness and kindness on to the people around us, and they would be happier and kinder, too. Simple as that. He said that this was the heart of Buddhism.

Well, over the years, that rocklike ball of anger first identified by Brother Damien had dissipated a good bit. I wasn't exactly ticked off at the world anymore, but unfortunately, I wasn't particularly happy either. I was just getting along. My anger had mellowed to what might best be described as persistent dissatisfaction. Some gloom, maybe. No matter where I went, what I did, I always felt a little bit empty. I have spoken to enough other people to know I am not alone in this feeling.

"Many of us worry about the situation of the world," Thich Nhat Hanh wrote. "We don't know when the bombs will explode. We feel that we are on the edge of time. As individuals we feel helpless, despairing."

I recognized more of myself in his description than I am comfortable admitting. The low-level agitation, the sense of just holding on, was familiar. Nhat Hanh said the answer was at hand, however— that relief from this despair was as simple as breathing.

BREATHING? IT SEEMED too simple.

Then I had this bright idea—the best way to learn about Buddhism would be to see it in action, the best way to imagine how it might fit into my hectic life would be to see how other Americans are fitting it into their busy American lives. I was always a big fan of quests and adventures, and here was a chance to have my own. Buddhism has long thrived in Asian-American communities, of course, but I was most interested in searching out the homegrown kind, the American Buddhism springing up among those with no Buddhist background. I called it my American Buddhism Project, and immediately subscribed to every Buddhist newspaper and magazine I could put my hands on. I imagined myself the Ponce de Leon of American *dharma*, and set off with pen and pad.

That was my idea.

And that's how I ended up, three months later, sitting on a round black cushion on Monkey Mind Mountain, trying my best not to scream and run off.

3

JUST SITTING

....

I Obsess a Lot, and

Then I Get Distracted

AFTER BREAKFAST ON Saturday, each of us at Zen Mountain Monastery is given a work assignment. Work, Jimon explains, is part of Zen practice, a way to integrate meditative concentration into our everyday tasks. It is also, clearly, an efficient way to keep the monastery clean.

Everyone works, we are told, from the lowliest weekend visitor like myself to the highest-ranking monk. Even the abbot of the monastery, John Daido Loori, works, though I don't see him sweeping floors anywhere near me. In fact, we have yet to see him at all.

I am paired with Tom, an affable glassblower from New Jersey, and we are instructed to merge our Buddha selves with a ten-pound bag of onions, to dice diligently until we completely fill a giant wooden bowl, and to talk as little as possible in the process.

Tom and I don't talk at all. We are high achievers. Instead, we chop like skilled chefs, running through the heap of onions in record time. And a lesson is learned. It is easier, more efficient, to chop onions when you are only chopping onions, not conversing, checking up on the rest of the kitchen, answering the phone, flirting with the young lady scouring the coffeepot, or whatever.

When done, Tom and I wash up the knives and cutting board with a bottle of Big Top blue dish detergent, and the head cook gives us a second chore: hauling a forty-gallon plastic garbage can of kitchen waste out to a well-composted compost pile the size of a Plymouth minivan. As a gardener, I am well impressed.

WHEN THE WORK is done, we return to the main hall, meditate some more, then have instruction in Zen painting, the practice of catching an image in a single brush stroke. The lesson is so brief that all we really learn is that Zen painting looks simple but is deceptively difficult. Then a quick lunch, during which Harold, at my table again, lets us all know just how much of what we are learning he knew already, and complains about his aching back. I've noticed over the course of the morning that he has developed a minor limp, and my compassion is tested. I don't much like the guy, and I'm of the opinion that he deserves a pain in the back now and then, but I'm also beginning to sense that this is not a very Buddhist thought.

THE MONASTERY BUILDING is an impressive maze of rooms and hallways, but they are mainly small and dark, so in the break after lunch, I head outside for some fresh air.

The Zen Mountain grounds include 230 acres of nature preserve, and though a sign has been posted on the main bulletin board warning us that a hungry bear has been spotted in the area, I don't see one.

Instead, after a ten-minute climb straight uphill past cabins that house some of the longer-term residents, I run into three whitetail deer—does, nice-sized, very much alert and mindful.

Mindfulness is what we are focusing on this weekend: the unwavering concentration that comes from stillness. When we are sitting on the *zafu* pillow, we should just be sitting. When we are chopping onions, we should be chopping onions only, right there, right then, at the chopping board, as if the onions, the knife, and our hands were all that existed. Later, as we return to our lives as doctors, lawyers, Indian chiefs, we should ideally bring that mindfulness with us as well, and as a result, we should be far better able to focus clearly on whatever task comes to hand. Mindfulness is the antithesis of Monkey Mind. Turtle Mind, maybe.

Or Doe Mind. The does are totally concentrated, it seems, on the sounds, the sights, the odors, that surround them in the woods, are absolutely focusing on the moment at hand, not worrying ahead to the next hour or the next day or whether they'll have the money they need for retirement. They are sniffing the tall weeds, looking for tasty clumps of grass, and listening sharply, ever alert for change or danger.

Just then, amazingly, I am mindful, too, for what seems like an uncommonly long time, as I do nothing more than simply watch them stray nearer and nearer to where I crouch frozen behind a small stand of dry late-autumn brush. Watching the thin, sleek, elegant creatures, I lose track of why I am there or where I am going. The winter sun is shining on my back, and it all feels rather magical.

I suppose it is a Zen moment, but the quibbling monkey voices in my head start almost immediately to ruin it. *How trite!* the monkeys giggle. *City boy merges with nature. He sees a few cute, dumb animals and imagines he has achieved some spiritual plateau. Had a cheeseburger lately, animal lover? Okay, bonehead, you paid your money, you saw the deer, now why don't you go write a poem about it.* If you haven't yet noticed, my brain is home to some particularly skeptical, sarcastic, and mean-spirited monkeys. Blame it on the nuns.

Distracted by all of this, and with my leg muscles beginning to ache, I shift my weight, snap a branch under my right foot, and the does are off like lightning into the forest.

Walking back, I am filled with fresh misgivings. Remembering the hyperactivity of my mind during morning *zazen*, my discourteous questioning of the Zen liturgy, my distinct lack of Buddhist compassion toward my fussy roommate with the bad back, my natural mistrust of all things spiritual, I begin giving serious thought to the notion that perhaps I am being a fool. This Project I have concocted may be dead before it even gets off the ground. Perhaps my true nature is too frantic, cynical, volatile, and mundane for anything good to ever happen.

Back at the meditation hall, though, on the pillow again for the afternoon session, I have a meditative breakthrough. After sitting for fifteen minutes in total stillness and total silence, looking at nothing more than the gray robe of the stick-thin monk one row of *zafus* ahead of me, thinking of nothing but my breath, I lose track. I actually stop thinking for a moment.

Then of course, I have this thought:

Look, I'm not thinking.

And the bubble bursts.

But for that brief fragment of time, there was no real time, because I was not keeping track, because I had forgotten to grasp greedily at every moment and analyze every twitch and twitter of my life, and it was a remarkable feeling.

I could very well have been spaced out on my *zafu* for an hour or more, though in all honesty it was probably no more than a few minutes. What I experienced was not *samadhi*, the Zen state of "no mind"—or maybe it was. But whatever it was, it felt good. And immediately I want to get the feeling back.

Wanting that feeling to return is attachment, of course, and Buddhists say that attachments are bad, that as soon as I attach to a feeling and pursue it, it will elude me all the more. Our minds are tricky. If we want something, we can't get it. Once we stop wanting it, it comes. This is why Zen is so hard.

I am not at all sure why I experience this mini-*samadhi*, if I may call it that. Perhaps it is just the wonderful excess of fresh, clean mountain air that I have inhaled over the lunch break, or perhaps it is a timely answer to the doubts that washed over me on my walk back down the mountain, or perhaps it is random and meaningless.

I just don't know, but during the instructional session that follows, I find myself sincerely wishing the various black robes would talk less and let me sit some more.

IN THE LATE afternoon, Jimon takes a seat at the head *zafu* to prepare us for face-to-face teaching by Abbot John Daido Loori. Loori, an American-born scientist and photographer, is founder and director of the monastery. The students call him Daido-shi.

I know all of this from the brochure that came when I registered, though I have yet to see the man, and face-to-face teaching, it turns out, is not so simple as going into a room and asking Daido-shi a question.

Smiling her lovely smile, Jimon tells us the rules:

During sitting meditation that evening, we are to listen for an announcement. When we hear a voice saying, "All weekend retreat participants who desire *dokusan* now enter the line," we are to spring from our *zafus* and race for the hallway just outside the meditation hall. First come, first served.

But this is just the beginning. Once we reach the hallway, we are to wait in line, sitting in half lotus or whatever position our legs are able to accomplish, until a bell is rung. That bell, coming from an inside room where Daido-shi is waiting, signals the first person on line to approach and enter his chamber.

When the first person goes into *dokusan,* the formal name for the face-to-face encounter, the rest of the hallway line moves up one space. When it is our turn, and we enter the *dokusan* room, we are to put our hands together, bow twice, then step forward, then bow again, then do a full prostration bow, dropping to our knees and bowing until our foreheads hit the floor, then another half bow, then we should sit about a foot from Daido-shi's knees and introduce ourselves, first name only, and tell Daido-shi what kind of practice we do ("If you don't know," Jimon tutors us, "just say that you count breaths"), and then we can ask Daido a question.

He will answer the question, or else he won't.

We can ask a follow-up question, perhaps, but as soon as Daido-shi rings the bell again, we are to spring to our feet, bow like mad, and get the heck out of there, because our turn is over.

"*Dokusan* is an important part of the teaching," Jimon warns us gently. "Don't waste this opportunity. Think, if you could ask a question of the Buddha, what would you ask?"

GEEZ WHEEZ, HOW intimidating. Daido-shi, we are told, has learned his Zen Buddhism from another teacher, and that teacher had a teacher before him, and that teacher can trace his Buddhism back to yet another teacher, and then another, and another, and another, centuries back, an unbroken string of face-to-face teaching, theoretically returning all the way to the historic Shakyamuni Buddha, also known as Siddhartha Gautama, the good fellow who started all of this. Direct transmission, it is called.

Zen is not learned from books, Jimon tells us, it is learned from teachers, and for a teacher to be legitimate, his or her transmission lines should be intact, and John Daido Loori is the real thing.

So because of this direct transmission, teachers of the lineage are sometimes referred to as "living Buddhas." *Dokusan* will be our chance to meet with a living Buddha, but we have to remember the rules.

The weekend training participants seem clearly unsettled by this prospect, and they pepper Jimon with worried questions. How exactly do we know when to get in the line? Which bow comes first? Are there two small bows and then a big one, or one small and then two big ones? What do we do after the third bow?

As for myself, I am beginning to feel skeptical again. Back in the old days, I never much liked the deference we were expected to pay our parish priests, or the idea that they were God's hand-picked representatives. They were just guys who had volunteered—I knew that, even as a kid. Anyone with a working brain had to question the idea that priests were special emissaries of God, worthy of so many exceptional privileges, because it was the priests themselves who had decided this, and kept reminding us of it. As the comedian says, isn't that a little too convenient?

So here is Jimon, touting Daido-shi's special standing in the Buddhist world, and it brings up all my deep-rooted cynicism. I haven't even met the guy yet, and I'm beginning to dislike him.

"Daido-shi is not a guru," Jimon says, as if reading my thoughts. "He is a teacher, with a deep understanding of the *dharma,* of the teachings."

Well, here is another fine Zen contradiction. If the man is not to be treated as a guru, why all the fuss, ceremony, and complex choreography just to ask him a question? I'm a college professor—I have office hours. Just knock on my door.

"Can we rehearse the bows?" a young woman named Connie asks.

"No," Jimon answers with her calm, quiet smile, a smile that I'm noticing is actually common among the black robes. "I don't think so."

We have an open hour before dinner.

Many of the weekend participants settle on the couches in the dining hall, busily reading magazines that have been left on a big table. Aren't we supposed to be emptying our minds?

Apparently not. One of the resident staff opens the Monastery Store, and we are allowed to do some shopping practice. The small shop is filled with books, tapes, clothing, incense, and Buddha statues. I am mindful of not buying too much, but come away with a nifty sweatshirt, a coffee mug, and two postcards.

Supper is black bean soup, salad, corn bread. One consistent aspect of the retreat is the excellent food.

Our dinner-table conversations are dominated by more nervous speculation and anxiety over *dokusan*. I can tell from the strained voices that many of my fellow newcomers are as confused and intimidated as I am. Eventually we move on though, to a discussion of our healthy, tasty meal, which segues easily into talk about our various obsessions with losing weight and our nasty eating habits back in our real lives.

A few of us have young daughters, it turns out, and weight and body image leads naturally to a discussion of Barbie dolls, and how it is that after concerted efforts to shield our daughters from the anorexic Barbie culture, they still come home one day wanting nothing more than tiny clothes and a pink plastic Corvette. Direct transmission, obviously. The teachings are directly transmitted from one four-year-old girl to another, in an unbroken chain of Barbie *dharma*.

LATER, WE SIT *zazen* again, and all I can think about is what I will ask Daido-shi, whether I will even get the chance to ask him anything, and whether his exalted self will immediately sense my wobbly soul and impure motives. I am ready to spring from my seat at the first hint that newcomers are being called to the *dokusan* line, knocking people over if need be, just to get it over with, so that I can concentrate on my meditation again.

But Jimon's voice calls new students on the north end of the meditation hall first. And, as promised, they *do* sprint. It is a full-out footrace, fairly dangerous on the slippery wood floor, and raucously loud. The springing and racing part is a disconcerting contrast to the slow, deliberate stillness that accompanies every other activity here, but Jimon said it is a way to show our eagerness.

I am stuck on my *zafu* listening to the bell ring, calculating by the bell's interval just how long Daido-shi is taking with each student, sneaking a peek to count the number in line, and quietly figuring the math of whether he will even get to those of us sitting on the south end. Not what the Buddha had in mind, probably.

To distract myself from my *dokusan*-anxiety, when I sense Jimon behind me, I bow, and slant my head to one side.

Thwack!

The pine *kyosaku* slams down on one shoulder. I slant my head to other side.

Thwack!

Jimon never mentioned the evening before that she was the one who would be wielding the *kyosaku* stick, but she is.

The points on my back where I have been struck burn, then ache, but it is very effective. I feel my obdurate, unyielding shoulders begin to melt down in a way they never have before. My body begins to relax, and my mind, well, it does, too, just a little.

SOMETIME LATER, ANOTHER announcement is made. "Weekend retreat participants on the south end . . ."

With every non-Buddhist competitive American Yankee Doodle capitalist fiber of my being, I spring and bound, overtaking five fellow students who are nearer to the line but slower getting up from the pillow, and end up in the *dokusan* queue with just three people ahead of me.

But then, before my turn actually comes, a different bell rings, signaling that time is up. Jimon instructs me and six disappointed newcomers directly behind me to return to our places in the meditation hall for the evening's closing ceremony.

And soon after this, we are back in our dorm rooms for lights out. The beds are small, uncomfortable, squeaky, the heat uncertain, the room frigid. I stare at the wire frame of the bunk above me for about ten minutes, frustrated and unsure why I ever thought I would want to spend a weekend with Buddhists, why I ever imagined Thich Nhat Hanh's advice applied to me, where I ever got the idea that a consummate unadulterated nerve-ending like myself could find peace anywhere.

Then I drift into the deepest *zazen* possible.

SUNDAY

The bell wakes us again before dawn. Harold dozes right through it, of course, snoring like a rusty sump pump, until Wayne compassionately shakes him awake.

Slipping on my new black ZMM sweatshirt, I notice out of the corner of my eye that the freshly awakened Harold's first act is to pull two rubber earplugs out of his ears. He heard my watch through ear plugs?

Breakfast is scrambled eggs and bagels, and once again everything tastes better than expected. Perhaps it isn't that the food is so awfully good—I mean, scrambled eggs are scrambled eggs. Maybe the truth is that all of this meditating does something agreeable to the taste buds.

After breakfast we have another hour of work practice. In my case, I do Scrubbing Out the Industrial Refrigerator *zazen*. It is a big refrigerator, a walk-in closet really, with crates of fresh produce and jars of various sauces. I mindfully remove all the food, take out the wire racks, wash the racks, wipe out the inside of the refrigerator with baking soda, clean the insides of the doors, replace the racks, replace the food, wipe off the outside until it sparkles. I am awfully proud of my work, but when I turn to the long-term resident who acts as crew chief, she unaffectedly tells me to sweep the dining room.

Apparently, no one here ever says "Job well done" or "You clean a refrigerator better than anyone, big guy." And perhaps that is deliberate. Perhaps I should be cleaning the refrigerator simply so that the refrigerator will be clean, not to prove what an anal-compulsive wonder I can be. No ego, no praise, no need for praise. Just a clean refrigerator.

DURING THE MEDITATION session that follows, I begin to notice much less pain in my legs and ankles, though they now tend to fall asleep faster. After the first thirty minutes of quiet sitting, we rise for a brief period of walking meditation. I stand, my legs numb and un-supportive below me, and lurch wildly forward, nearly toppling two senior students who seem in no way amused.

I have been obsessing off and on about *dokusan* again, but not quite as much as the evening before. Shortly after we finish walking and sit again, a voice calls "all those participating in the training weekend who have not yet sat *dokusan* may now . . ."

Bouncing from my *zafu* as if my buttocks were metal springs and sprinting for the line once more, I come in second, just behind

Wayne. I sense my competitiveness is not pure Zen mind, but they *did* encourage us to hurry.

The bell rings. I am at the front of the line for three minutes, while Wayne has private face-to-face teaching, and then the bell rings again. It is my turn, finally.

I stand and enter the *dokusan* room, do a series of bows, though not the series we were taught, then totally forget to introduce myself or to mention what sort of practice I am doing. ("I obsess a lot," I would have said. "Then I get distracted.")

None of this matters, however, because Daido-shi isn't even looking at me when I enter. I could have done an Irish jig with my tongue out. Eventually though, sensing my presence, or smelling my fear, he looks up from his meditative reverie. At first, his meticulously shaved head and ornate chestnut robes, as well as the exotic trappings of the *dokusan* room, make him seem vaguely Asian, but he is not, and once you look closely, the fact is obvious. He is a large man, tall and big-shouldered, American, and I spend a moment ruminating as to whether he looks more like the actor Telly Savalas or the actor Ernest Borgnine.

He smiles a very warm, very sleepy, amused smile, and I wonder if he's reading my mind.

"Do you have a question?" he asks.

I spit out what I have silently rehearsed: "How do I diligently pursue what Zen has to offer, without grasping?"

It seems like a dumb question before it is even off my lips.

"Just sit." He smiles with his eyes, then nods.

The response seems too simple, so I repeat the question, trying somewhat different words but asking essentially the same thing. "How can I be deliberate about seeking Buddhism and yet not be too attached?"

"Practice is enlightenment," Daido answers this time. "Enlightenment is practice. Just sit."

He flashes his beatific smile again. Though I am trying, he is fairly hard not to like. When I attempt to ask the same question a third time, however, he shakes his head and rings the bell—the signal that the face-to-face teaching is over, for me at least.

I spring up, still unsure how many bows I am supposed to do, but no matter—despite all our preparation, he isn't watching.

PRACTICE MAKES PERFECT. Is that it? Is that my message from the Buddha-heir?

In Zen, it begins to seem, simplicity is profundity. That is a hard concept for someone like me to accept, though. Perhaps I have seen too many New Yorker cartoons about going to the mountaintop and learning the meaning of life from the meditating mystic. I thought Daido-shi would say something profound.

He probably has.

OUR FINAL LUNCH, oddly enough, is spaghetti with meat sauce. But this is an American Buddhist monastery, so why not?

Harold does not sit with the rest of us at the newcomers' table. He is across the room, at a table dominated by monks and long-term monastery residents. Perhaps he is offering to teach them a thing or two.

And perhaps he is the reason I must come back.

It occurs to me that I have focused far too much on my snoring, limping, bragging nemesis this weekend, and not enough on myself. Whatever brought me here, whatever precipitated my brief spiritual foray, that ball of dissatisfaction that has lingered on since Brother Damien called me a rock, is probably all tied up with this—with my critical Monkey Mind voice, and my facility for blaming everyone else.

Before I can wonder any more about that, lunch is ended, we rinse our dishes, and my first Zen Retreat weekend is unceremoniously brought to a halt. There is nothing to do but drive home.

Just sit, Daido-shi told me.

For the next six hours, I do, because I am stuck behind the wheel of my car. I sit and wonder.

What would Brother Damien say?

4

ZEN GARDENING

Me and My Green-Thumbed Monkey

ONE ADVANTAGE OF visiting Zen Mountain Monastery is that pure peer pressure keeps me on the round black cushion for the better portion of every day. Surrounded by Zen professionals, with the outside world nearly shut off, I am clearly no Buddha, but I am at least sitting.

Following the retreat, though, I return home. With my daughter off to first grade and my wife busy teaching dance classes, I have the whole house to myself, free to meditate mindfully for hours, but instead, every distraction imaginable is right at hand, and I succumb. The computer; the television; the radio; the refrigerator; the ability to stand up, walk outside, and check whether the overnight ice storm has ripped off my gutters—the combination of these proves far too compelling.

At first, I try to sit for fifteen minutes, then ten, then five, but even that measly amount becomes altogether impossible. It seems inconceivable to me that I really meditated for six hours a day on Tremper

Mountain, willingly and, to a certain extent, successfully. Did I merely dream that?

If anything, the experience has whetted my appetite to learn even more, to try harder. I keep remembering my mini-*samadhi*, and wanting it back, so much so that I consider hiring someone to stand guard over me, to exert the needed peer pressure, and maybe to whack my shoulders with a stick now and then. But fat chance even that would work.

The problem is clearly inside. My mind is a monkey, and the monkey needs Ritalin.

Yet I am stubborn. I try everything. I purchase a *zafu* for my home, and set up a small Buddha altar with fresh flowers and green silk. My resolve lasts through the weekend.

I try meditating in the car, turning off the radio, not thinking about my destination, what I will do as I burst into the office, but instead just breathing along the road. This could potentially be dangerous if I were to achieve another sudden Zen state, but I am nowhere close.

I try meditating in the bathtub. I fill the porcelain *zendo* with warm water, submerge myself up to the ears, so that all that really pokes above the surface are my toes, a bit of my Buddha belly, and my nostrils. I breathe, and the water blocks out every sound. I have constructed a poor man's sensory deprivation tank, and though it is calming and I have my best luck at actually achieving some semblance of stillness, my monkey brain reprimands itself once more —*How pathetic, this is the best you can do? I've met calmer two-year-olds.*

By mid-month, I am squeaky clean but have otherwise lost all vestiges of my brief Zen training. I try one night to mindfully slice an onion, but my rice begins to stick, the spinach boils over, the phone rings. My wife calls to me from the living room, "Did you mean to leave your socks here?"

STILL, IN THE midst of all this chaos, a seed of understanding begins to form. This inability to focus, this always being somewhere other than where I am, is surely somehow connected to my never being satisfied, and together they probably form the heart of my predicament. It is not just the absence of God in my life that made me investigate this new old religion, but an overall sense that some *thing* is missing. I have become like a compulsive eater whose belly never feels full. Only it is not my belly that seems empty.

Like most of my friends and acquaintances, I have built up some modest success in my life. I have managed somehow to form a relationship with a wonderful woman, even to let her, against all my better judgment, talk me into having a kid. I have subsequently fallen so deeply in love with that kid that the experience has redefined my whole sense of what love means. I am at a place now where I have a reasonable mortgage on a comfortable house, a secure job, my family is happy, and I don't wake up in the middle of the night wide-eyed and worried that I will be homeless or penniless anytime soon. But still, what's the point?

At times, it seems as if the only real point is to somehow keep holding it all together. Life becomes a loop of concern and uncertainty.

NOT KNOWING WHAT else to do, and having no Buddhist friends to whom I can turn for advice, I settle for buying another book.

Bookstores, you may have noticed, are full of guides to Buddhism, to Zen, to mindfulness, and to spirituality in general. These books have become a cottage industry of the 1990s, though it is not so clear if anyone actually reads them. I think baby boomers just feel calmer having them on the bedside table.

I manage one evening to shut down enough of the outside distractions, however, that I can actually read one of my purchases—*Zen Mind, Beginner's Mind*, by Shunryu Suzuki. The back cover tells me that the Japanese-born Suzuki is founder of the first Zen training monastery in America, so I hold out hope that he will address some of what is bothering me.

Early on in the book, Suzuki talks about "mind weeds," all those distracting thoughts that make meditation so difficult. Well, obviously, I can relate.

But these weeds, it turns out, are not bad. Just as garden weeds, when properly composted, can be used to nourish the vegetable patch, Suzuki writes, mind weeds, when properly observed, can nourish a beginner's Zen practice. Watch the weeds, he advises, be aware of them, watch them begin to lessen, and that will give you hope.

"If you have some experience of how the weeds in your mind change into mental nourishment," the old monk promises, "your practice will make remarkable progress."

So here I am, it seems, with a mind full of dandelions and crabgrass, worrying about it, and once again missing the whole point. Weeds are good. Weeds aren't what's stopping me, it's just my Monkey Mind insisting that weeds are somehow bad. If I let the monkey pronounce me an abject failure before I even begin, what chance will I have against him? These monkeys are so tricky.

It is exactly how Daido-shi said, apparently. Quit worrying so much, and just do it. Just sit.

Now I see.

The difficulty I have with Buddhism is that it's just too damn simple.

5

WHY DO TIBETANS HAVE SUCH TROUBLE WITH THEIR VACUUM CLEANERS?

They Lack Attachments

FROM WHAT LITTLE I understand of Buddhism at this point, it seems certain that it is not supposed to be competitive. Yet I am an All-American boy, raised on sandlot baseball and Monopoly, and in the end the idea of fighting against and maybe someday conquering my screaming Monkey Mind is what primarily keeps me going.

Buddhists come in different types. Just like Catholics and Methodists and Baptists all believe in Jesus but differ on some finer points of theology, the varying forms of Buddhism essentially embrace the teachings of the first Buddha but diverge from there. American Buddhism, I learn, falls into three main categories—Zen, Theravada, and Tibetan. Maybe what my Project needs is to sample all three. Maybe it's time to try another approach.

In Atlanta, while attending a conference of writing teachers, I hear about Losel Shedrup Ling, a Tibetan Buddhist community holding a weekend retreat, and call for directions.

I am told to find the La Hacienda Condos, out along Jimmy Carter Boulevard, in suburban Norcross. When I get there, however, and find myself surrounded by pseudo-Spanish townhouses and pink and white azaleas, I'm convinced some mistake has been made. Then I notice that a fair number of the cars scattered about sport red-and-yellow FREE TIBET bumperstickers.

More incongruous even than the condo complex is the clubhouse where the retreat is held. The large commons room has rustic wood siding, dreadful yellow-and-orange shag carpeting, and a billiard table. There is a swimming pool just outside, visible through large windows. If I wanted something different from John Daido Loori's dark, ominous monastery, I have surely found it.

The crowd here is young. They wear tight jeans instead of sweat-pants, which strikes me as a bad idea for sitting meditation, but they look good, and they have better tans, certainly, than anyone at Zen Mountain.

In the back of the room are plates of cookies and fruit. I pick up a fudge-striped cookie, and a thin woman in her forties wanders to where I stand, introduces herself as Susan.

"Is this your first time?" she inquires.

"Well, no. I've been to a Zen retreat."

"Oh, you have?" She looks out at the swimming pool, as if expecting to see someone she knows. I follow her gaze, but all I see is water.

"Will this retreat be much different?" I ask.

"Oh," Susan warns, "Tibetans are big on teaching."

THE BILLIARD TABLE has been pushed to one side, making room for about thirty-five maroon cushions. A makeshift altar has been set up and elaborately decorated in the front of the club room, and after we are instructed to take our seats, the teacher, Geshe Lobsang Tenzin Negi, comes in and sits beside the altar.

Geshe-la, as the regular students call him, is a Tibetan monk. I learn from the brochure that Geshe is a title, somewhat akin to Doctor of Buddhist Philosophy, and it means he has undergone a rigorous course of study, starting at age fourteen. He is now roughly thirty-six, but looks younger.

He starts us off with a twenty-five-minute guided meditation— "guided" means he talks us through it, encouraging us to relax our minds, to let go of our thoughts. He takes our monkeys by the hand, so to speak.

Then he clears his throat and begins the teaching. "This evening," he says, "I will be speaking on the 'Three Principle Aspects of the Path to Enlightenment.'"

At Zen Mountain, we sat like Buddha statues, stiff and unmoving, while the various monks and senior students instructed us. Here, though, as soon as Geshe-la launches into his teaching, most everyone begins rooting around in their purse or backpack, searching for a scrap of paper, a pen, a notebook. My jaw drops to the floor.

I dig out my own pen and start scribbling. The first of the Three Principle Aspects of the Path to Enlightenment, Geshe-la tells us, is "a longing for freedom from problems."

Okeydoke, I think. I qualify. I would be hard-pressed, in truth, to think of anyone who didn't want freedom from problems. Though I'm pleased to have fulfilled the First Principal Aspect, I'm unfortunately having a fair bit of trouble picking up the soft-spoken monk's ensuing words, because the room's central air unit is cranking along like a freight train.

Most of us are seated on the maroon cushions, but a few folks with weak knees or weak resolve are in folding chairs halfway back.

After about five minutes of strained listening, and goodness only knows what I missed and how it might keep me unenlightened, one of those chair-sitters, a middle-aged fellow with thinning hair and a muscular build, gets up, finds the switch, and turns the air off.

I wheel around on my *zafu* and offer him a smallish bow of gratitude. *Gassho,* my friend.

He smiles and returns my bow.

WITH THAT, I can hear perfectly. Geshe-la is explaining that the source of our problems is our human weakness, and that weakness is our tendency to become attached. Attached to all manner of things.

Geshe-la explains it this way:

Though we often tend to blame them, it is not external things like families, jobs, or money that create problems for us in our lives. Rather, what actually makes us unhappy is our tendency to desire that these things bring us happiness. This expectation that family, job, money, a new car, whatever, will make us happy is what binds us and causes our discontent.

In other words, by expecting these things to deliver lasting delight, we are setting ourselves up for a fall. We think, "As soon as I get that new job I'll be happy," then we get the job, our joy is fleeting, we start to feel unfulfilled again, and suddenly we are miserable. All of our expectations have been dashed. Maybe we need a new job? And the cycle continues.

It is the same thing with marriage—we expect marriage to make us happy, it does for a while, then our old problems creep up again, and we think, "Gee, I guess I married the wrong person." This, too, can become an unhappy cycle.

Geshe-la nods, smiles, then translates his lesson into a metaphor. Think about ocean water, he says. Just as there is nothing wrong with "things," he explains, there is nothing at all wrong with ocean water. "It is what it is—ocean water. But if we drink ocean water in an attempt to quench our thirst, it will kill us."

In other words, it is okay to have a suburban home, an air-conditioned Lexus, a comfortable income, it is even okay to deliberately arrange our lives in such a way that these things become possible, but only so long as we don't expect these things to make us happy. Happiness is internal, not external, and chasing externals is a waste of time, a cycle of longing, an endless wandering in the wrong place after the wrong thing. Buddhists call it *samsara*.

I call it "feeling vaguely dissatisfied." Geshe-la, it seems, has put his finger on my problem.

GESHE-LA FIDGETS in place, arranges his orange robe over his left shoulder, clears his throat.

"Now I will talk about how to overcome this longing," he announces, and suddenly I am on the edge of my cushion.

"In order to free ourselves," Geshe-la explains in his slow, careful diction, "we need to overcome our emphasis on this life, and then overcome our emphasis on next lives."

Huh?

As if he has heard my unspoken grunt, the monk smiles and repeats his answer: "In order to be free of longing, we need to overcome our emphasis on this life, and then overcome our emphasis on the next lives."

My Monkey Mind slips on a banana. I mean, the words make sense, and Geshe-la expresses himself in complete, grammatically correct sentences, but what is he saying? If I don't emphasize this life, what do I emphasize? What does it mean to emphasize this life anyway, or the next?

I am all akimbo with questions, but Geshe-la just goes on. His discourse becomes circular, or perhaps it just seems so because my mind is somersaulting in place back where it got stuck. Suddenly, I can't even take notes, because I am locked into a cycle of trying to make sense of the statement that came just before the one I am only half hearing.

I can't read minds, so I can't say if others in the room are following Geshe-la any better than I am, but I do notice that the level of fidgeting picks up considerably. One woman reaches for her nasal spray, another decides it is time to borrow a working pen, a third seems to be nodding off.

(At a later point, I will ask some people more familiar with Tibetan Buddhism, and they will confirm that the casual atmosphere that has surprised me so much here is not particularly out of the ordinary. Tibetans, they tell me, are looser than Zen practitioners about nearly everything, except the need to memorize vast amounts of material. "You may have noticed how hyper Zen folks are about keeping their *kesas* clean," one fellow tells me. A *kesa* is a monk's outer robe. "Well, I once saw a Tibetan monk blow his nose on his.")

Geshe-la rocks on his cushion, gestures like my Italian in-laws, and as his *kesa*—his outer robe—keeps slipping off his shoulder, he keeps pushing it back up. He never quite makes clear, to me at least, what "emphasizing this life" means, nor does he say anything to clear up what it means to overemphasize the next life.

While I wrestle with my bewilderment—"attached" to his words, expecting them to bring me enlightenment—he somehow reaches the end of his talk.

"Craving something good and hoping to avoid something bad is what creates problems," he says in summary. "So get rid of all attachment *and* aversion."

UNLIKE MY EXPERIENCE at Zen Mountain, this is not a residential retreat. We do not sleep in dorm rooms and wake in the morning for more instruction. We drive home, and in my case that means braving the six southbound lanes of Interstate 85, returning to the clearly nonmonastic Atlanta Renaissance Hotel.

Before long, I am standing in the hotel lobby, right outside the Georgia Ballroom, where a band called Yuppie Scum is playing rock 'n' roll oldies. I'm sipping a beer with my poet friend Tony. We are both leaning on a wall, trying to look young, lean, and single, instead of middle-aged and married.

We aren't having much luck.

About this time, an auburn-haired, distinctly beautiful young woman walks by in the sort of exceedingly tight red dress that can make a man's heart do the hokeypokey.

"*Oooooooh,*" Tony moans. It is the moan of a middle-aged married man.

"What's wrong?" I ask.

"That." He nods toward the young woman. "What would your Buddhist friends say about that?"

Well, of course, he shouldn't have asked.

"Buddhists," I explain earnestly, "would point out that the only problem here is *your* discontent. It is not the beautiful young woman walking by that makes you yearn and suffer, but what you do in your mind as a response, the thoughts that you form. You construct a cycle of *samsara*—'Oh, she is so lovely, oh, I will never sleep in her bed, oh, life isn't fair, monogamy is cruel, oh, I'm miserable.' The Buddha, however, would say, 'Oh, how wonderful that I get to see such a beautiful young lady. Oh, isn't she nice, so shapely, and aren't I lucky to have witnessed her walking by. Oh, what a beautiful flower.'"

Tony gives me a distinctly queer look, as if I've sprouted long orange hairs on my forehead, then wanders off toward the bar, no doubt looking for someone far less sanctimonious.

• • •

THE YUPPIE SCUM are a bit much on the heels of Tibetan philosophy, so I retreat to my hotel room and read some materials I gathered off a table after Geshe-la's talk.

Tibet, a small country in the Himalayas, has been occupied by China for the past forty years or so. The Chinese don't call it occupation, of course, they claim an historic right to the land, but according to human rights observers, the Chinese rule has led to the torture and death of 1.2 million Tibetans, many of them monks and nuns, as well as the destruction of thousands of monasteries, including Drepung Loseling Monastery, from whence Geshe-la's lineage derives. The seat of the native Tibetan government, and much of the monastic activity, has moved south, out of the country, into India.

One result of the Tibetan troubles is that a growing number of Hollywood celebrities like Richard Gere and Uma Thurman are putting their names behind the cause, and one reason perhaps that the crowd at Geshe-la's retreat seems younger than the students at Zen Mountain Monastery is that a host of MTV grunge rock bands have embraced Tibetan freedom as well. Beastie Boy Adam Yauch wrote a song called "Bodhisattva Vow," which ended up on the hip hop/punk band's album, *Ill Communication*. Yauch also took a small group of Tibetan monks along on the band's big Lollapalooza tour a few years back, where many teens and twenty-somethings first had their awareness raised.

In June 1996 Yauch helped organize a two-day Tibetan Freedom Concert in San Francisco's Golden Gate Park, with regular reports on MTV and a sell-out crowd of fifty thousand per day. Headliners such as Smashing Pumpkins, Red Hot Chili Peppers, Sonic Youth, and (for the older crowd) Richie Havens and Yoko Ono helped promote the Free Tibet cause; and, in addition to the music, there was a monastery tent, a sand mandala, a political action tent, and lots of encouragement for young concert-goers to boycott Chinese goods.

Chinese goods are not so cool right now. The Tibet Support Group, I learn from one of my newly acquired brochures, encourages us to not buy anything marked MADE IN CHINA because the repressive Chinese Army owns many of the nation's manufacturing plants, uses imprisoned political dissidents as slave labor, and employs the profits to expand the war machine.

We tend to imagine that Buddhists sit under trees and just breathe all day, but life for Tibetans is not nearly so simple.

SATURDAY

The next morning, I am back at the La Hacienda Condo clubhouse, milling about and sharing in the bagels and jelly. The pool table is now garlanded with flowers.

The fellow who took it upon himself to switch off the air conditioning in our first session wanders over, introduces himself as Pete. "Thanks for affirming my actions last night," he says.

"Thanks for shutting the damn thing off," I answer. "I couldn't hear a word."

Pete and I chat awhile. He is a carpenter, a fact born out by the thickness of his forearms and solidness of his shoulders, and is in his forties. "I'm coming to this out of Christianity," he tells me, and because of the way he says it, or perhaps just because I am guilty of stereotyping Southerners, I suspect he means *Christianity*—the serious type, not the Sunday morning variety in which I was raised.

"A big difference," I offer.

"Not really," Pete points out. "There are lots of parallels."

"The Golden Rule?"

Pete nods. "It's basically the same message," he says. "Jesus was a Buddha."

• • •

CLEARLY THE LOSEL Shedrup Ling people have shed their attachments to punctuality. Though the retreat is scheduled to start at 9:30, we don't get the signal to sit down until about 9:46, and much to my continued amazement, people bring their coffee cups right to the cushion. If this had happened at Zen Mountain, John Daido Loori would have flipped his wig (if he weren't bald). No one even sneezed in the Zen Mountain *zendo*. Here in Atlanta, one fellow actually brings his paper plate to the *zafu* and munches on a bagel while we wait for Geshe-la.

It takes about five minutes for everyone to settle in, and then a phone begins to ring incessantly, back by the kitchen. No one answers it.

We just sit. Not meditating really, because some are reading, some are eating, and I am craning my neck out toward the pool to see if perhaps the Geshe is taking a morning swim.

Near ten, someone I don't know announces, "Sorry for the delay, we are having trouble locating Mike."

It was nice of him to explain, though I haven't a blessed clue who Mike might be. It occurs to me that maybe Mike was supposed to drive Geshe-la in this morning, and perhaps it was the Geshe himself on the phone, wondering if we had forgotten him.

By ten-fifteen, I am getting aggravated—I paid for this retreat, got up early, braved Atlanta traffic. Everything in Buddhism, though, seems to come back to a lesson. Clearly, it is my desire for things to be a certain way that is making me unhappy, my insistence that Geshe-la follow a certain set of behaviors. It is not his tardiness that causes my distress—it is my reaction to it, and only I can control my reaction. So, I am responsible for my own unhappiness.

Ba-da-boom, ba-da-bing. Momentary enlightenment.

• • •

DURING THE LONG wait, my fellow retreatants are popping up like toast, shuffling, rearranging, wandering to the back of the room for more tea, but Geshe-la does finally arrive, seeming a bit flustered.

We stand when he enters.

"Have a seat," he says softly, shyly.

We sit.

He leads us in meditation for fifteen minutes, a meditation that Geshe-la describes as "Kalmnez Abie Ding." I assume these are Tibetan words, perhaps extremely sacred Tibetan words, and speculate as to what they might mean instead of focusing on my breath as I should be. It is only when the meditation ends, and Geshe-la repeats the phrase, that I realize that all he said was "calmness abiding." Oh well.

WE WHIP OUT our notebooks. Class has begun.

Geshe-la begins with the second of the Three Principle Aspects of the Path to Enlightenment: "We Do It for Others."

We seek enlightenment, he explains, we strive to become Buddhas, not for our own glory or pleasure or bliss, but for the benefit of all sentient beings. If we are enlightened, we can help lead others out of suffering, and into their own enlightenment, perhaps devoting our lives to teaching others, as did the original Buddha and the many teachers who have followed. We can't, in fact, become enlightened for our own glory, edification, or welfare, because there is no "us," in Buddhist terms.

Which is actually the Third Aspect: "Realization of Emptiness."

"We do not exist as independent concrete beings, as 'I' and 'them,' rather we are all the same," Geshe-la explains.

What follows is a brief lesson in yet another of the basic Buddhist principles—nonduality. Nonduality is the opposite of duality—

duality is the mistaken notion that the ten thousand things in the universe—that chair, that bird, Newt Gingrich—truly are distinct and separate. Buddhism argues that they are not, that they all exist in the mind, the mind that sees them, registers them as objects or concepts. If these things are in our minds, they are us. And if we are all in one another's minds, we are all one another.

Understand?

I'm not sure *I* do, frankly, but above and beyond the philosophical, one everyday manifestation of this is the understanding that "others" do not make you mad. For instance, I said to my wife the other day, "You are driving me up a wall," then realized, thanks to my nominal meditation practice, that it is my wall, and I'm the one climbing it, so I guess it isn't her fault. When I explained this, she was so grateful, she wanted to send Geshe-la some money.

IF YOU ARE of my generation, meaning that your mind is slightly addled from teenage marijuana abuse, the concept of total oneness of all things might bring to mind part of a lyric from the Beatles' *Magical Mystery Tour* album: "I am he as you are he as you are me and we are all together."

John was clearly thinking of nonduality when he wrote this lyric (and was perhaps smoking pot as well). As you may remember, John, Paul, and the boys had a weighty flirtation with meditation back in the early 1970s. It wasn't Buddhist meditation, though, it was Hindu, as taught by the Maharishi Mahesh Yogi. Though there are clear similarities, and Buddhism and Hinduism flow out of the same early Indian source, they are indeed different.

Likewise, the orange-robed, bell-ringing, shaved-head Hare Krishnas you used to see in most airports weren't Buddhists either. In our Western ignorance, we often lump them all together and get them confused.

We also have a bad habit of looking on all Eastern religions as "cults," though these religions are in many cases far older than Christianity, often with more adherents, and usually there is very little that is cultish about them. Though the shaved head of a Zen monk might set off warning signals in a parent's mind, the truth is, Buddhism is far from cultish—it often downplays the importance of the teacher, and sometimes even leaves open the question of whether it is the right path.

As a Catholic, it was pounded into my brain day after day that I belonged to "the one, true faith." Buddhists, on the other hand, tend to say, "Well, here is a way, not *the* way, but a pretty good one. See if it works for you."

BACK TO GESHE-LA. This third aspect, "the realization of emptiness, our lack of an independent existence," is also the essential meaning of the Buddha's teaching, he tells us. Once we realize that we are empty, that what we call our "self" is really just a bag of meat supported by calcium sticks, and that all energy is all energy, a continuum of energy, and that there is no independent "I," no "us and them," no "if he has it I can't have it, and if I have it, they can't," kindness and compassion can only follow.

Aware of my lack of an independent existence, how can I mindlessly squash a bug? The bug is me. How can I pop off a middle finger at some guy who cuts me off in Atlanta traffic? The guy is me. The finger is me. Heck, the traffic is me. How can I not do whatever is needed to aid the homeless, the hungry? We are all one thing.

But contrary to the shallow "Hey dude, like there is no me, there is no you, so maybe I can borrow your car and sleep with your girlfriend" sort of interpretation that flourished in the sixties, the Buddhist realization of our lack of independence actually calls for greater responsibility. For ourselves—first of all. And ultimately, for everyone else, everything else, because we all rise and fall on the same wave.

JUST WHEN I flatter myself that I'm starting to grasp the heart of it all, Geshe-la calls me back to earth.

"All of this talking, this is not really Buddhism," the Tibetan monk reminds us. "You can get instructions for swimming, but if you want to learn to swim, you have to get into the water."

For a moment, I hope that he is going to compel us all into the pool out back, but time is running short.

"My retreats are talking retreats primarily. I talk into enlightenment." Geshe-la grins and his audience laughs with him. "Time permitting, we should be meditating, but unfortunately we do not have the time." He pauses to think. "You should spend the time on your own to meditate and deepen the experience."

He pauses again.

"Of course, your concentrating and deep listening is a form of meditation . . . but perhaps I am only trying to justify myself."

He started late, probably gabbed a bit more than he intended, and has run over the allotted three hours. It is a refreshing apology, and I realize Geshe-la may be more like me than he is like the Buddha, which is fine. I tend to trust someone who makes a few mistakes and apologizes more than I trust someone who seems always to be right.

THE RETREAT ENDS on that note, and twenty or so minutes later I am pulling into the parking lot of the Georgia Antique Center and International Market, a suburban flea market in Norcross, in hope of finding some cobalt blue vases for my non-Buddhist wife. Renita is very attached to her David Austin roses, and the vases will display them nicely.

The large building has everything, from a small store selling nothing but Coca-Cola paraphernalia to shops offering rebel belt buckles, Confederate flags, and rude T-shirts, from antique stores with lovely oak tables and turn-of-the-century glassware to shops brimming with the tackiest modernist mirrored furniture imaginable. The flea market, it also turns out, houses an Asian knickknack shop, filled with plates, and fans, and wooden fish, and little porcelain Buddhas.

I buy a Buddha figurine for my dashboard, to keep me safe on my drive home, then turn to study a table covered by beautiful silk wall hangings. The prices, ranging anywhere from $3 to $20, are amazing, especially when you consider the wonderfully intricate hand embroidery.

The shopkeeper senses my interest and wanders over.

"Nice, no?"

"They are wonderful," I say, and pick one up to inspect it more closely. "I can't believe the prices."

He smiles and nods. "China," he announces proudly.

I screw up my eyebrows. "Pardon me?"

"Made in China," he explains. "Where else do you get such cheap labor?"

My mind fills with thoughts of Tibetan dissidents forced into slavery by the Chinese military, and suddenly the embroidered silk is not so much a bargain. I drop the banner as if it were covered with mealworms, head for my car, and leave the shopkeeper shaking his head.

PART 2

PRACTICE MAKES PERFECT

6

CATHOLIC BOY ZEN

....

Was Jesus a Bodhisattva?

DRIVING HOME FROM Atlanta, it hits me—my first experience with Tibetan Buddhism was basically a six-hour sermon.

Six hours.

And I sat through it, willingly.

Six hours?

As a kid, I would have cringed at the very thought. Even Father O'Donnell's shortest orations, as little as fifteen minutes on those Sundays when his colon was acting up, made me squirm and moan. In my Catholic-boy mind, the sermons were endless, irrelevant, and insincere. Not only were they like medicine—ill-tasting and suspect, forced upon me by a condescending adult—but to the best of my knowledge, they didn't cure a thing.

So I ask myself, why was I sitting on an uncomfortable cushion, listening to Geshe-la for hours on end, and not complaining? When I didn't have to? When no one, not even John Daido Loori, had threatened me with eternal damnation?

AS SERENDIPITY WOULD have it, soon thereafter I catch word of Father Robert Jinsen Kennedy.

Kennedy is a Jesuit priest, which explains the "Father" part. He is also Irish-American, which explains the Kennedy. Finally, he is a Zen teacher, and "Jinsen" is what the Zen people call a *dharma* name. It means "Fountain of God."

My childhood was filled with more Irish-American priests than a Bing Crosby movie, and the idea that this one could be a Catholic clergyman *and* a Zen teacher makes my mind reel.

For a while, when first hearing about him, I assume he is an *ex-*priest, but this turns out not to be the case. Father Kennedy is still a Jesuit, and given the growing list of questions in my mind, I know I have to talk him.

So I drive to Jersey City, New Jersey. Kennedy lives in the Gothic Towers Condominiums, an old but dutifully maintained brick apartment complex. When St. Peter's College needed what was once the priests' rectory for classrooms and offices, they moved all the clergy, lock, stock, and chalice, into the condos, and various Jesuits share one of the upper floors. In addition to their apartments, the floor has been converted to include a dining hall and a chapel.

On the first floor of Gothic Towers, the priests have a few small meeting rooms, where I suppose they hear confessions or counsel the grieving. Father Kennedy and I meet in one of these rooms.

He is white-haired, trim, and dressed casually in a green shirt and tan pants, and has blue eyes that seem unusually clear and attentive. His gentle smile and calm manner put me at ease almost immediately.

We shake hands and exchange pleasantries, and I open with the obvious question. "You are still a priest, a Catholic priest, but you teach Zen?"

"I'm a Jesuit," he explains, "and many Jesuits, as we go to foreign countries, try to learn something and bring it back to the Church. I saw this wonderful Zen tradition in Japan, and as a Jesuit, I thought, this should be available to everyone."

It was the Jesuits, in fact, that sent Father Kennedy to Japan in the 1960s, where he met the Zen teacher Yamada Roshi, a man who, according to Father Kennedy's book *Zen Spirit, Christian Spirit*, "radiated an enlightened and fruitful life, and to my delight . . . accepted me as his student, a Christian and a complete beginner who knew nothing at all."

Father Kennedy sat in meditation with Yamada Roshi for some time, then later completed his studies back in the United States, with Bernard Tetsugen Glassman. Ironically, Glassman, the teacher who finally "transmitted" the teachings to Kennedy, is himself a Jew, and counts among his students a reform rabbi, a Roman Catholic nun, and a Muslim sheik.

Now, Kennedy is a fully "ordained" Zen teacher, with his own body of students. This is apart from his duties at St. Peter's College, where he teaches Japanese language and theology. And also apart from his *third* job—Father Kennedy has a private practice as a psychotherapist, with an office across the river, in Manhattan. He is a busy man, and not a simple one.

"You keep active?" I say, pointing out the obvious.

Father Kennedy nods, then sits back, looking infinitely placid, as if he has nothing better to do than spend the entire day talking with me. Surely he must have thirty other things on his slate, but he doesn't let on in the least.

He explains that he has a number of students who come to him for Zen training. A handful of these students live nearby, and other groups he meets with weekly, monthly, or sporadically, in Virginia, Baltimore, over in Greenwich Village, and in upstate New York.

"Are your students Catholics, or Buddhists?" I ask, still trying to make sense of what seems like too great a contradiction.

He nods and smiles. I get the sense from him that every question I ask is just the right question. "By and large they are practicing Catholics who also do Zen meditation. But that's not my business, that's the individual conscience. I just help them sit."

None of his business? I thought it was precisely a Catholic priest's business to make sure we were all Catholic. It is the "one, true faith" after all, unless the nuns were lying to me.

All the time Father Kennedy talks, my Monkey Mind is in overdrive, still puzzling over the riddle of why I willingly sat still for Geshe-la's lengthy sermon. It occurs to me that I am perhaps exhibiting a form of reverse prejudice. Most of my parish priests were middle-aged Irish guys who smelled like booze—in other words, just like my dad and my uncles. Am I therefore imagining the Buddhist teachers to be more wise simply because of their exoticism?

Or maybe I respect Geshe-la because of his simplicity. When I was growing up, priests drove better cars than my parents, lived in far nicer quarters, and even had servants, old Irish widows who kept house and cooked the food for a pittance. The priests were princes, and usually acted like it.

Or perhaps the truth is a combination of message and messenger. No matter how much he talked (and talked and talked) about Christian kindness, Father O'Donnell ruled his church, school, and parish like a petty tyrant, seeming always on the verge of an indignant discharge. Geshe Lobsang Tenzin Negi, however, seems content, truly gentle, as if perhaps he practices what he preaches.

My childhood view of God, unfortunately, was not much better than my view of his messengers. Thanks to the constant warnings of the nuns that "He always knows what you are doing, even what you are thinking," God seemed to me to be little more than a vengeful,

CATHOLIC BOY ZEN 61

mind-reading Santa. He knows if I've been naughty, he knows if I've been nice, he knows if I've had evil thoughts, and he's keeping track until the end of time. Perhaps that is why I'm finding myself suddenly drawn to the more-benevolent Buddha.

Finally, Father O' Donnell didn't in any way seem to lift our burden—he seemed in fact to substantially add to it. On those rare Sundays when I did pay attention to what he had to say, I was routinely paralyzed between fear and guilt. "You are a greedy little child, and you are going to end up in Hell because of it." Geshe-la's sermon, on the other hand, made my burden seem lighter, or at least tried to suggest a way that the burden-lifting might happen. In my experience, Catholicism seems focused on what we do wrong, what we will do wrong, and the bad things that will probably occur as a result, whereas Buddhism seems more clearly focused on the positive in us, and how to bring that positiveness more forward.

I try to phrase all of this in a question to Father Kennedy, and end up stuttering and babbling and feeling foolish, but he nonetheless seems to understand.

"I think many people felt the experience of their early Catholic upbringing was somewhat negative," he reassures me, nodding sympathetically. "I think that's where the Church was at at that time."

I interrupt, feeling bad that this priest might think I am lumping him in with the black-cassocked villains of my youth; he doesn't seem anything like them. "I'm not asking you to be an apologist for my Catholic upbringing," I say. "Maybe mine was worse than others? Maybe it was just the particular school I went to?"

"But I would agree with you," he insists. "Many people feel like you do. We did have in this country, perhaps because of our immigrant status, a sort of punitive, defensive attitude, but we're trying to work beyond that."

He seems to reflect a moment, then continues.

"Of course, Catholicism asks different questions than the Buddhists ask. Catholicism is not just a wisdom tradition for a few contemplatives, you see. We have a billion people out there we are trying to educate and move along, so there is a different perspective."

Emboldened by his willingness to address the possibility that Catholicism is not all love and kindness, I advance another observation. "Buddhists seem more open to doubt," I suggest. "When I was in Catholic grade school, I was the one always asking too many questions and getting in trouble for it."

"Yes," Father Kennedy concurs. "That's certainly part of the problem. We tried to put God on a blackboard, into a very simple answer. We had all these children, and all these nuns trying to teach all these children, and we simplified, we simplified God into a lovable simple commodity, the good and gentle Jesus and so on, when actually life is terrifying."

LIFE IS TERRIFYING sometimes, especially to the young.

First grade, in fact, was all about fear for me. It was frightening enough to be away from home, but Good Shepherd Catholic School was staffed almost entirely by the Sisters of St. Joseph, and back in those days these were frightening women. I remember them all as being large, which isn't surprising since I was only six, but I remember them as being even larger than other adults, larger certainly than my mother. In those days they wore thick black habits from head to toe, interrupted only by the stiff white bibs and the starched triangles that seemed to cut right into the forehead. Sister Mary Catherine's job was to beat me into submission, to make me a quiet and obedient Christian child, and she did so with a single-minded purposefulness.

I don't remember a whole heck of a lot of what the nuns taught us about God, except that they seemed to be in fear of him just as I was in fear of Sister Mary Catherine. I remember—maybe in first grade, maybe in second or third—a long discussion in religion class about whether it would be all right for a starving woman to steal a loaf of bread from a bakery truck if she were stealing it only to bring it to her starving children. This was a Catholic school *koan*—Thou Shall, after all, Not Steal—and I remember our bright little minds wrestling with this for hours upon hours. Certainly, one of us insisted, it is not a sin if she is only feeding her starving kids. We weren't exactly starving in my small Catholic parish—most of our fathers had manual labor jobs in the forges and foundries up along Twelfth Street—but it wasn't a big stretch for some of us to imagine it.

"Well certainly she wouldn't be punished for that," we insisted, but with a question in our little voices.

The nun seemed truly troubled. She didn't want to break down and admit that sin was circumstantial—goodness only knows what can of catechismic worms that might open—but she saw our point. "Well," she finally demurred, "it would only be a venial sin anyway, and you don't go to Hell for a venial sin."

My early religious training was very much all about Hell—getting there or the avoidance of getting there. Hell, Hades, Satan's Inferno, the fiery underworld—whatever your terminology—was a vivid place, with skin being ripped away by fire, hot lances puncturing flesh, and an endless stream of misery and regret. A nice thing to teach kids.

So, our future was clearly terrifying. One slipup, the slightest weakness of character, and we might burn baby burn. And meanwhile, we had our temporal lives to worry about. In too many cases, our second-generation blue-collar fathers were stumbling drunks, often on the verge of losing their horrific factory jobs, sometimes hitting our moms, or hitting us, or ramming their 1958 Plymouths into poles. Our older brothers were going to Vietnam. Life was not a McDonald's commercial.

Buddhism, I am beginning to think, addresses suffering far better than most Christian churches. My Buddhist teachers—Daido-shi, Geshe-la, and through books and tapes, Thich Nhat Hanh and Shunryu Suzuki—all seem to acknowledge that life is difficult, and discontent is endemic, but if we work at our lives, take a little control, we can make it better, even make it good.

The nuns, on the other hand, kept reminding us that Jesus had died so we could be happy, so if we weren't, then we were surely ungrateful little wretches. We were encouraged to feel awfully damn guilty about this every moment we could.

"God is good," we were told over and over growing up, yet all we had to do was look around to see some not so good stuff. The single most prominent icon of my youth was the crucifix above the blackboard at the front of every classroom, and in those days, Catholic crucifixes tended to be very realistic, down to every last nail, every last blood drop, the wide gash in Jesus' side. I mean, God let *that* happen to his son, and we were supposed to trust in his goodness?

Father Kennedy talks about suffering in *Zen Spirit, Christian Spirit*, pointing out, for instance, that the United Nations estimates the number of starving children at forty thousand a day. "That means that each day, forty thousand mothers beg God for bread and water for their children and their prayers are not heard," he writes. "Let those of us who are well-fed pause to grasp this terrible reality."

God's judgments, if that is what they are, are harsh, perplexing, and not, on the surface at least, always very compassionate. And Kennedy adds, "It is sad that organized religion, which should open us to and prepare us for this awful mystery, is instead so fussily pedantic. It is equally sad that organized religion domesticates and dwarfs God to a controllable and lovable size."

In other words, the Catholic Church, faced with the daunting task of teaching deep spiritual mysteries to millions upon millions of ragtag children, took the easy way out—they made it black and white, absolute good versus absolute evil, and turned basic Christian theology into a comic book with superheroes (God, Noah, Jesus), villains (Judas, Satan, Pontius Pilate), and the central premise that supernatural powers were all that could save us.

This is me speaking now, not Father Kennedy, but I think he might agree. The uncomplicated comic book version of a merciful all-powerful "SuperFather" who knows all, sees all, and somehow directs all works well if you are between the ages of five and maybe twelve, but as we get older, start asking deeper questions, start reflecting on the serious inconsistencies of life, it is no mystery why so many of us drift away from the Church.

Granted, it is easy to bash Catholics and Christians for their failings, and it would be massively naïve of me to imagine that the various Buddhist schools aren't guilty of similar distortions or misdirection. Like so many Americans now giving Buddhism a test drive, my search is tainted to some degree. I am not just studying a new religious path, but am also reacting, maybe overreacting, against what I see as an earlier, ineffective spiritual upbringing.

Father Kennedy's approach is to merge the two, the old faith and the new, suggesting that Zen meditation and mental discipline can be excellent techniques for attaining a deeper Christian conviction. Other Buddhist teachers, most notably Thich Nhat Hanh, the Vietnamese monk whose taped voice first reignited my interest in Buddhism, take it a step further.

In his book *Living Buddha, Living Christ*, Nhat Hanh suggests that "When you are a truly happy Christian, you are also a Buddhist. And vice versa." He also points out that the Christian concept of the Holy Spirit, the anointing energy sent by God, bears a striking similarity to the Buddhist idea of awakening and enlightenment.

And like many others, most recently Pete, my Christian carpenter friend at Geshe-la's Atlanta Retreat, Nhat Hanh draws a parallel between the words of the Buddha and the most basic teachings of Jesus. In the end, he asks, how much difference is there between the Buddhist principle of kindness and compassion toward all sentient beings and the Christian Golden Rule, "Do unto others, as you would have others do unto you"?

Nhat Hanh's comparisons rely not on centuries of structured religious interpretation, but on Jesus' own utterances. In his book, he quotes this New Testament passage: "Thou shalt not kill; and whosoever shall kill shall be in danger of the judgment. But I say unto you, that whosoever is angry with his brother without a cause shall be in danger of the judgement . . . whosoever shall say, 'Thou fool,' shall be in danger of hell fire."

Contained in that small scriptural excerpt are two key Buddhist precepts—right action and right speech—and also the notion of *karma*. Moreover, Nhat Hanh points out, "Jesus did not say that if you are angry with your brother, you will be put in a place called hell. He said that if you are angry with your brother, you are already in hell. Anger is hell."

Jesus, Nhat Hanh is suggesting, is talking about the mental formations that bind us, the negative effects of our own negative thoughts. These mental formations are exactly what Geshe-la was talking about in Atlanta. They are Suzuki's mind weeds. They are the negative monkey thoughts that keep us miserable when we have so much.

THOUGH NHAT HANH does not go so far, others have made the claim that Jesus was himself a Buddhist, or at the very least, that the historical Jesus may have been influenced by Buddhism, that he may have encountered Buddhist thought at some point in his early life (the historical Buddha predates Jesus by five hundred years), or that he may perhaps have come across a Buddhist teacher. What was he doing for those forty days and forty nights in the desert? To some, it sounds a lot like a meditation retreat.

"Have you heard this?" I ask Father Kennedy.

"Oh, yes," he answers, and doesn't recoil one bit.

Though he strongly doubts that Jesus himself had any occasion to cross paths with a Buddhist, the Jesuit does allow for the possibility that one of the gospel writers, the men who translated Jesus' message, may have read some Buddhist scripture. "The Gospel of John," he explains, "was written in Alexandria in a time when Buddhism was known to be there."

Then he laughs. "Of course, the emphasis now is to say that Jesus was a Jew, not a Buddhist."

"Everyone wants him," I laugh back.

THE IDEA THAT Jesus was a Buddha is blasphemy, of course. The Pope certainly doesn't buy into it, and I doubt Jerry Falwell or Pat Robertson likes the idea.

Nor does my curiosity toward Buddhism, Father Kennedy's pursuit of Zen, Richard Gere's preoccupation with Tibet, or the interest of the hundreds of thousands of other Americans who are attending retreats, buying books, or learning to breathe mindfully from Thich Nhat Hanh's tapes meet with the approval of everyone in the West. Some, in fact, see it as a very dangerous trend. Christian bookstores are filled with warnings against New Age religions, even the very ancient "new" ones.

My wife, Renita, teaches modern dance, and a few years back, when we lived in Louisiana, a father rushed in one day to pull his daughter out in mid-lesson, because, he explained, modern dance is "too much like yoga," and of course, yoga, based on Hinduism, is the posturing of the infidel.

In Central Pennsylvania, not far from my current home, a group of angry parents recently stormed a school board meeting because some teachers were offering deep breathing to their students as a way to relax before a difficult math test.

"Breathing is Buddhist," one of the mothers told me. "We are very Christian here."

Well maybe breathing *is* Buddhist, but try going a few days without it. We all could do with some good deep breathing, it seems, and any way you look at it, the ancient Asian tradition is making serious inroads in America.

In Father Kennedy's opinion, this is exactly where it belongs.

"Yamada Roshi felt that Zen was dead in Japan," Kennedy tells me in the Gothic Towers conference room. "He felt that Zen's future oddly enough was not in Japan at all, but here."

"He said that?" I ask. The wheels in my Project Mind are turning rapidly. This is exactly what I was seeking.

"I have met many wonderful, educated Japanese for whom Buddhism is just a word," he explains further, "they know nothing about it. So I think the future for it is here."

In Father Kennedy's vision, the new American Zen will not be so caught up in Asian ritual, not a mimicry of the Japanese rendering. "The very meaning of Zen is not to imitate anyone, because there is nothing to imitate, but to be yourself, so it is rather silly for Americans to continue to imitate Japanese, or Tibetan, customs," he admonishes. "We respect our teachers and respect the forms that they bring, and we keep them up to a certain extent, but always it has to be an integration with the present moment. Why keep alive a certain form that existed in the thirteenth century in Japan?"

Much more so than the good folks at Zen Mountain Monastery,

Kennedy is already Americanizing his teaching. He doesn't hold *dokusan* but grants his students a "private interview," and he substitutes English words for the Japanese wherever else it is feasible.

"We cannot just imitate the Japanese. In fact of all people, the Japanese are the most unique, the most inimitable, so how can we imitate them? We just make ourselves look silly."

I think back to my *dokusan* bows, and wholeheartedly concur.

I FIND MYSELF liking Father Kennedy more and more the longer we talk, and wishing I might have found a gentle, wise, supportive, willing-to-entertain-doubt priest such as this when I was younger. Who knows, I might still be Catholic.

But I still don't get it. Which is he? How does the personable Father Kennedy wear both hats, the Catholic and the Buddhist?

"Are you actually a Buddhist?" I finally ask.

"No," he clarifies. "I just did the Zen training. You don't have to be a Buddhist to do Zen. What I try to do is take the contemplative tradition of Zen Buddhism and find that it parallels our own Christian tradition, so that we can enrich each other."

In other words, he practices basic Zen, the long hours of contemplative thought and mental rigor, yet believes in the Christian God and in Jesus. I point out to him the obvious—that he is in a tricky spot. The Pope himself has issued clear warnings against too much acceptance of Eastern religion.

"Well I think that is the place for Rome, to issue warnings," Father Kennedy says, "and certainly Zen is not without its dangers. If Christians are not well formed in their faith and then they wander into a Zen center, they could easily be blown away. So is there a danger? Of course, but there is danger everywhere."

How about Buddhists, I ask him, how do they feel about his balancing act?

"This is a touchy point," he admits, "because many Buddhists feel you must be Buddhist because Buddhism nurtures Zen, Buddhism is integrally connected with Zen, but you do not have to be a Buddhist to see into your own nature, and that's just a fact."

Can you be both? Are these traditions really compatible?

"Well it can be done," he says, pointing to himself. "But it is not for everybody. Zen is not for all Buddhists, and it is certainly not for all Christians. But for those Christians who are drawn to this, they can do it without renouncing their faith."

Are any other Catholic clerics doing what he does, I ask, teaching Zen to other Catholics?

Kennedy knows of one other still-practicing Jesuit in Texas, Father Ruben Habito, who is a Zen teacher, and also a nun in Baltimore, Sister Janet Richardson. "But there aren't that many of us," he says with a shrug. His eyes twinkle. "That's one of the things that make it so exciting."

BEFORE I LEAVE, Father Kennedy gives me the grand tour. First he takes me onto the roof of the Gothic Towers, and points across the river to the Manhattan skyline. "There it is. Babylon."

He laughs, but I think he means it.

Then he takes me down the elevator again, to see the chapel, and then the small apartment he shares with another Jesuit. A tiny room off the kitchen has been converted for private interviews, with mats, cushions, a *kyosaku* stick. The *zendo,* where he and his students meditate, is one half of the room he uses as an office. The room is filled with books, a chess set, some chairs, *zafus,* and a beautiful Buddha-face statue. Off that room is a small bedroom.

He takes me to the priests' cafeteria for coffee. We sit across from one another, and he looks at me deeply, calmly, generously, and smiles. "Was there anything else you wanted to talk about?" he asks.

It has been over twenty years since my last confession, but suddenly, unexpectedly, I am unburdening myself of all my confusion, my fears—about Buddhism, about having left the religion of my youth, about all manner of things. The words just pour out of me. He is a Catholic priest, and I am asking his forgiveness.

And I feel guilty, telling this kind man that I no longer consider myself Catholic, that I am not even sure I believe in Jesus—well certainly not in the Catholic sense—but he just nods. He reassures me. He reaches across the table and pats my shoulder.

Later, Father Kennedy shakes my hand, and we part company.

I am off to Babylon.

7

YOU CAN CHANGE YOUR MIND

....

And Your Karma, Too

IT IS A hot, muggy Saturday in Babylon, the water vendors
are doing a land-office business, and Buddhists with lawn chairs,
pillows, Igloo coolers, box lunches, and all manners of practice are
spilling into Central Park.

Two canopy tents have been assembled in a quiet wooded green
near the Rambles, a short walk from the Metropolitan Museum of
Art. Around midday, a large brass gong resounds 108 times, signaling the start of the third annual Change Your Mind Day, a mini-
Woodstock for meditators.

While the audience settles onto the lawn, various monks, nuns,
and lay practitioners take their places on a stage of wooden plat-
forms, and eventually Soto Zen priest Pat Enkyo O'Hara grins in our
direction.

"You might be more comfortable if you have a blanket to put
under your butt," she instructs, "but any way you sit is fine." She is
on crutches, so, for her at least, full lotus is out of the question.

O'Hara talks us through a body-awareness meditation, and though it is hard staying mindful with in-line skaters whizzing past and mounted police clip-clopping along the walkways, we give it our very best shot. Some of us sit formally, others sit casually, and a few smear on suntan lotion, then fall back on their towels so as to be thoroughly mindful of the sun's rays.

Helen Tworkov, editor of *Tricycle: The Buddhist Review,* the sponsor of the day's events, sits center stage in a flowing white outfit, and after O'Hara finishes, she welcomes us. "There is something interesting going on in American Buddhism," she says. "We have Sri Lankan teachers, Tibetan teachers, Japanese teachers, American teachers, and they are all represented here today."

As if to prove her point, the area behind the stage fills with monks, a rainbow of robes—orange, yellow, burgundy, red, brown, gray, black. In the background, what sounds like Hare Krishna chanting wafts through the trees—there is another, unrelated event happening down the hill.

Tworkov points out the happy coincidence of this. When the historical Buddha first got started in India, she explains, he probably heard similar chanting in the background. We all nod and grin at one another. An omen?

The lawn is rapidly filling up. If there was ever any doubt that stressed and jittery America is experiencing a surge of interest in Buddhism, the doubt is dispelled here.

IN THE NEXT forty minutes or so, we hear from Lobsang Tamten, a Tibetan from Philadelphia; Master Sheng-yen, from the Ch'an Meditation Center in Queens; and Ven. Kurunegoda Piyatissa, from the New York Buddhist Vihara, each giving us their slightly different slant and chant.

More people fill in gaps in the lawn, and the crowd stretches to nearly one thousand people who seem eager, willing, and, for the most part, hip in a New York sort of way. It is a Soho crowd, with some West Villagers thrown in: young, fit, healthy, most wearing casual but stylish clothes, a few in bikinis, and at least one man in a black suit with a cane and bowler hat. A bodybuilder cuts across the lawn with an orange cat on a leash. Someone's cellular phone goes off. Instead of incense, my nose detects the sweet scent of cocoa butter.

The day before, Father Kennedy told me that "the very meaning of Zen is not to imitate anyone, because there is nothing to imitate but to be yourself."

We are American Buddhists, being ourselves.

There are even a few children present, which interests me, since I saw no children at Zen Mountain or the Atlanta retreat. I have my own young daughter, who I have not brought with me, and I am beginning to form my own vague fantasies about someday introducing her to Buddhism and contentment. Most of the kids here, though, seem fairly bored by all the meditation, chanting, and speeches.

One kid is trying to peel up a lump of thick grass with the front shovel of a yellow Tonka earth scraper. "Don't pull that out," the kid's father instructs. "Be kind to the earth."

DURING A BREAK in the formal presentations, I get up and wander back behind the big blue tents. It is the staging area for monks and musicians, and to my surprise I see John Daido Loori from Zen Mountain Monastery back in the shadows, circled by a few of his senior students. I debate with myself whether to drop over and say hello—I mean, it is not as if he would remember me or anything—when I realize why he is lurking backstage instead of sitting on the main platform—Daido-shi is sneaking a smoke.

A monkey runs screaming through the jungle of my mind. At

ZMM, the teaching monks stressed to us that Daido was a direct *dharma* heir, the nearest thing to a living Buddha, yet here he is, cigarette in hand, bending over and cupping it slightly, as if he were a tad self-conscious, or maybe embarrassed. In fact, he looks like a very big, bald-domed high school kid in Zen robes, hoping the principal doesn't look out her window.

Ah, but here I am forming mental attachments again. No one ever promised that my Buddhist teachers would be saints. There are revered teachers throughout Buddhist history, in fact, that had drinking problems, or a weakness for sexual indiscretion, and even a few who were thought to be insane. The Buddha, after all, was human, not a god. If we weren't all imperfect, why would we be seeking perfection?

DAIDO-SHI DOES TAKE the stage soon after, though, and instead of a sermon or sacred intonation, he fields *dharma* questions from the audience at large.

"We have a microphone here," he instructs the growing crowd. "It reaches pretty far. You can say what you want to say, I'll respond, you may respond, and this can go on back and forth for a short bit. If you are satisfied, you can say 'Thank you for your answer' and that will conclude it. Or, if you just want to get out of it, you can do that too, and if I want to get out of it, I will say 'May your life go well,' and that ends it."

He grins, the crowd chuckles. Daido-shi has a wonderfully easy presence.

"By the way," he asks. "Has anybody changed their mind yet?"

A few hands shoot up.

"Good."

Daido has one microphone, one of his students walks through the crowd with a second. He fields a few common, basic Buddhist questions easily, questions he has probably addressed hundreds of times in *dokusan*, then a young man takes the microphone, announces that he is a New York University student, and begins a monologue.

"Hi, um, I came out here today, I think it's really great," the young man says. "I think it's great to see a lot of people out here for spiritual awareness. Um, I think in many ways you all came out for many of the same things, we're out here because we're all very much in tune with spiritual objectives, and I think that's beautiful."

The crowd starts to giggle. This kid sounds stoned. His voice drips with insincerity, like some *Saturday Night Live* parody of a Buddhist lounge act. ("I just flew in from Tibet. Boy are my arms tired.")

The kid keeps talking.

"I feel God has blessed everybody, he's blessed this day for us, and I think it's a great thing. I think Zen is a great philosophy. I studied it a little bit. I admire it for the, um, kinda the in-tuneness with yourself, and you know, the exercise of getting to know yourself . . ."

Daido leans into his mike, grins his Cheshire grin. "May your life go well," he says.

The young man looks confused, and there is a small cheer from the crowd. Off to one end of the lawn, I spy Boris, a fellow student from my ZMM retreat. Boris stood out that weekend because he always seemed to be scowling, slumping in his chair, or otherwise looking displeased. Today, he is slumped on the lawn, seeming half asleep, but he sees me, too, and we exchange waves.

A blond woman in her late twenties takes the mike, asks Daido, "What is your question?"

"I don't know," he responds. "What is your answer?"

The crowd roars. We are having fun with this. The mike moves along.

"Hi," a young man shouts. "I have a question. If during *samadhi* you experience the falling away of body and mind, what experiences the falling away of body and mind?"

Samadhi is the Zen state where concentration becomes focused and the separation between "self" and everything else seems to disappear. The young man's question is another fairly basic one, circular as it is, because Zen teaches that there is no self, that the concept of "self" is really a trick of perception.

"When you achieve *samadhi,* there is no experience," Daido answers. "There is no witness anymore, and there is no way to even know that *samadhi* took place, other than the passage of time. If you started sitting and it was morning and a second later it is mid-afternoon, that's called *samadhi.* Coming out of that *samadhi* is a kind of freshness to things, and the mind begins to function in a very different way. It's no longer locked into that self-centered reference system, and that's usually where realization takes place, at the edge of coming out of deep *samadhi.*"

My hat goes off to Daido-shi. I have been busy listening to talks and tapes and reading more and more books, and this is one of the clearest, least mystical explanations of enlightenment I've seen or heard.

JOHN GIBSON OF the Philip Glass Ensemble plays soprano sax for the happy swarm, then tai chi teacher Maggie Newman—a lovely gray-haired woman with the grace of a ballerina—leads the crowd, perhaps 1,500 people by this point, in a series of gentle movements, and what results is a massive, vibrant dance, all these attractive, clear-eyed people waving their arms.

The sight is captivating. Even the venerable Beat poet Allen Ginsberg is on his feet, swaying like slow-motion seaweed, and a field of energy fills the lawn. I can hear my Monkey Mind and the Monkey

Minds of the multitudes saying the same thing over and over, "I should have brought my video camera, I should have brought my video camera."

But even I begin to relax eventually, enjoying the billow and surge. I look overhead, and sure enough, a white heron is circling. Another omen?

I'm not sure yet, at this point of the journey, whether I can rightly call myself a Buddhist, but I am feeling awfully damn happy.

AND CONFUSED, TOO. My experience at Zen Mountain Monastery was on the severe side, and though the atmosphere at Geshe-la's Tibetan retreat was certainly lighter, it was still a lot of work to follow his lecture. The activity in Central Park, on the other hand, ranges from good fun to downright silly. I have begun to imagine myself making progress on my self-styled Project—the search for American Buddhism—but I'm not sure where all of this now fits in. Is Buddhism in America the real thing, or just shallow amusement?

A few days after Change Your Mind Day, Helen Tworkov agrees to meet with me and talk some of this over. Her magazine is not the only American Buddhist periodical—there are plenty—but it is the largest.

Tworkov, a small woman with whitish blond hair, is a daughter of the Abstract Expressionist painter Jack Tworkov. She speaks with a passion, leaning forward when she makes a point, and is definite in her opinions.

The first issue of her magazine hit the stands in 1991. "We were going to print five thousand initially, and ended up with a first printing of seventeen thousand. That number has gone steadily up every single print run, and we are now printing about fifty-five thousand copies," Tworkov explains, seeming more mystified than pleased.

It is a beautiful, glossy quarterly. The graphic design alone is worth the cover price, in my opinion, but the articles are well written and well edited, too.

I now eagerly subscribe, but who is buying the other 54,999 copies?

"That's a little more uncertain," Tworkov smiles. "In the old office we actually kept a map with little stickpins in it, to see who was reading. The Bay Area was by the far the largest, and of course the New York area, but then there were these amazingly surprising pockets—we had twenty-one initial subscribers in South Dakota.

"Very quickly, within two or three issues, we had subscribers in every state in the region."

Why the growing popularity of Buddhism? I ask.

"I think the Dalai Lama has had a great deal to do with that," she answers. "He is a household name, everybody in this country knows who the Dalai Lama is, and there is a lot of respect for him. There is also the celebrity thing—people like Richard Gere."

I mention the recent spate of television commercials. To me, it seems, every time I turn on my TV I find some Buddhist reference. In a recent ad for Danka fax machines, a gray-suited Westerner crawls up a Himalayan peak, sees a smiling monk, says (groan) "Hello, Dalai," and asks for the "fax of life." There is a Gatorade spot showing the Bulls' Michael Jordan running to the mountaintop, again searching for the meaning of our existence. IBM and Apple have aired similar ads, and a recent commercial for Tic Tac breath fresheners features a wide-eyed blonde instructing us to "take a breath."

Tworkov laughs, points out that Christian symbols are "in," too. "Just look at any Madonna video."

We agree that spirituality in general is becoming more visible. But why?

"I think there is a sincere panic," Tworkov suggests, leaning far forward. "About the world. About the environment. About violence. I think there is a very sincere anxiety. You know, for a long time you didn't see people in their twenties coming into the *dharma*. In fact, there were moments in the mid-eighties where you looked around the *zendos*, or any kind of meditation hall, and you saw all of these middle-aged people, and you could have thought that Buddhism was going to die by attrition in this country. And that's changed.

"In Buddhism we talk about the mind that abides nowhere. The homeless mind, the mind that's not attached, the mind that's not dependent on a home, or a country, or nation, or money, or job, or status, for its essential identity. And a lot of what I get from talking to people in their twenties who come into Buddhism is a sense that they *literally* do not have a home. Their parents are divorced, there is a tremendous sense of fragmentation in families. I talk to kids coming into Buddhism who don't know where their mother is, don't know whether she's living on the East Coast or the West Coast, haven't seen her for twelve years or something. We have these amazing stories that we are all aware of. In a way it is a very sophisticated, a very evolved understanding. They take one look around and see that their last shot for any kind of security, or equanimity, is totally inside, because everything around them is falling apart. Their families are falling apart, their society is falling apart, and they see that they can go with it, and just fall apart too, or they can try to pull themselves together, and the only place to go is an entirely interior place. There is simply no outside place, they can get absolutely no footing outside. There is no sense of family, no sense of community."

Is the American Dream falling apart?

She nods. "I think it is extremely hard to kid yourself about it these days. I think you have to be verging on some sort of a psychosis to actually think that the American Dream is being held intact. Just read *The New York Times*. You don't have to be a rocket scientist to figure that out. The news will just blast you away."

I have come prepared to discuss the superficiality of our attraction to Buddhism, the lack of seriousness, but Tworkov surprises me with her answer. Maybe there is more to it than I have seen.

She surprises me, too, when I ask about her views on the state of American Buddhist practice. She wrote a 1989 book on this subject, *Zen in America*, has practiced Buddhism for decades, edits the largest American Buddhist magazine, and somehow, when I ask her views on American Zen at the close of the twentieth century, I expect her to lead the cheer.

She doesn't.

"Zen is a highly monasticized tradition," Tworkov answers. "But clearly, people are not interested in monasticism in this country at this time. I think it is questionable if you can take Zen out of the monastery, yet develop a secular context that can give it the same potency. Other people, which is mostly the American view these days, argue that there is a kind of equivalency, that Buddhism can be as strong in lay life as it can be in a monastery, that these are like two feet of the same body.

"I don't know which is correct. I do know that if Zen is to thrive in a secular society with any of the potency that it had, it has to create very new modes. In a way, right now we've managed—in my view—to disembowel it, without re-creating a strong secular content.

"For instance, I don't have any problem with meditation for stress reduction, as long as there are people somewhere in this world that understand that meditation is not *just* for stress reduction."

We are talking in the *Tricycle* office, on Van Dam Street in Manhattan's Soho district, a generous loft space divided by thin walls and rough metal shelving. As Tworkov's little wiener dog Max scratches at my socks and the staff busily assembles the fall issue around us, I ask Tworkov if she thinks there are strong American teachers; teachers that she feels are keeping the true Zen alive, at a pure level?

"I think there are some good people out there," she answers, "but very few that I feel unequivocally positive about. I know very few teachers who actually feel that they have attained what their own Asian teachers have attained, which I think sets up a real problem for them, as well as their students. Most of the teachers I know are painfully aware of the limits of their own understanding. They see this degeneration or devolution in three generations—their teacher, themselves, and their students. What are their students seeing, what do their students have to learn?

"I think the Asian teachers brought with them a monumental, almost a genetic history, and you can't pick it up that fast."

She smiles, leans back. "And of course," she acknowledges, "The Tibetan teacher Gelek Rinpoche once said 'You can never step into your teacher's shoes. Never.' So in his view, it has been going downhill since the time of the Buddha."

BACK IN CENTRAL Park, Ginsberg takes the stage.

The poet traces his Buddhist lineage back to the "dharma bums," poet-philosophers such as Jack Kerouac and Gary Snyder who helped turn a whole generation on to the *dharma*. Ginsberg, a self-described "flaky Buddhist," in a seersucker sport coat, white pants, and red suspenders, looks frail and thin, gray-bearded and wobbly, and it strikes me that the famous Beat poet isn't likely to "Howl" about anything today, except maybe Social Security cuts.

But my ability to be wrong knows no bounds. Accompanied by saxophone and guitar, Ginsberg rips into New York governor George Pataki, Newt Gingrich, Bill Clinton, Bob Dole, and just about everyone else in public office.

His voice is strong, musical, full of fire.

He half-sings, half-recites a poem called "Ballad of the Skeletons":

Said the Presidential Skeleton
I won't sign the bill
Said the Speaker skeleton
Yes you will

Said the Representative Skeleton
I object
Said the Supreme Court skeleton
Whaddya expect

Said the Military skeleton
Buy Star Bombs
Said the Upperclass Skeleton
Starve unmarried moms

Said the Yahoo Skeleton
Stop dirty art
Said the Right Wing skeleton
Forget about yr heart

The audience claps and laughs, filled with Ginsberg's piss and vinegar. I am watching one of the mounted New York police officers assigned to guard us. His horse is shuffling around on its front legs, dancing maybe, and the cop seems to be having a good time. Ginsberg sings on:

Said the Gnostic Skeleton
The Human Form's divine
Said the Moral Majority skeleton
No it's not it's mine

Said the Buddha Skeleton
Compassion is wealth
Said the Corporate skeleton
It's bad for your health

Ginsberg's folkie voice cracks occasionally, but he spares no one, sticking his sharp-pointed pen into right-to-lifers, pro-choicers, homophobes, tough-on-crime Democrats, think-tankers, multinationals, the World Bank; howling at the media, the advertisers, couch potatoes, talk show hosts, newscasters, even himself.

Later, Ginsberg does a version of the song "Amazing Grace," with revised lyrics calling for compassion for the homeless. He reads a few more poems, without the horns or guitar backing him, and then, "because it sounded so pretty," does "Amazing Grace" once again.

Maybe Buddhism doesn't always have to be sedate.

I THOUGHT GINSBERG would be the highlight of my day, but it turns out to be Michael Roach, an American-born, Irish-faced, burgundy-robed, grinning Tibetan monk from New Jersey.

He is a scholar of Sanskrit, Tibetan, and Russian, as well as a teacher of Buddhism. He trained at the Sera Mey Monastery, one of Tibet's oldest, now in Northern India because of the China problem. Roach heads the Asian Classics Input Project, an effort to transcribe ancient, sacred Buddhist texts onto CD-ROMs. He is a very bright man, and very funny.

He has come to Change Your Mind Day to demonstrate an old Tibetan custom called Geshe Debate. "The Buddha said, no one should follow Buddhism just because he said so," Roach tells us. "He said, anyone who wants to be a Buddhist should learn to reason and learn, to figure out why something is true. He encouraged his followers to question, to thrash it out."

So, much as it has been done in Tibetan monasteries for centuries, Roach and two young Tibetan monks, Ngawang Thupten and Jampa Longrey, thrash out the meaning of "karma."

"Today it is the Americans versus the Tibetans," Roach shouts to the large crowd, "so you need to help me. If my opponent makes a mistake, I will start a sort of Bronx cheer. I want to go over it with you, to make sure you help me at the right time." People are sitting up, moving closer to the stage, coming around from the back, grinning from ear to ear. They can tell that Roach is up to some mischief.

"The Bronx cheer goes like this," he says. "*Dooooooooh-chett!*"

It is fairly hard to describe the sound he makes, a sort of Tibetan catcall. The *Dooooooooh* part slowly rises from the back of the throat, growing louder and higher in pitch. The *chett* comes fast, as if spit off the tongue.

We try it two or three times with him.

"*Dooooooooh-chett!*"

"*Dooooooooh-chett!*"

"It means, You really screwed up," he explains. "It means, What a stupid thing to say."

Everyone laughs but the two young monks. They don't seem to understand a word of English.

Roach removes his robe from his shoulder as a sign of respect. "But that's about the last polite moment in the debate," he warns us, then claps his hands together, swings his *mala,* a wooden rosary, in the direction of the young Tibetan visitors, and shouts questions, alternating between the Tibetan and English languages.

"What is *karma*?" he asks. "What is the essence of *karma*?"

The monks and Geshe Roach shout back and forth in Tibetan.

Roach claps his hands sharply. The monks shout out more answers. They seem concerned and worried.

Roach turns to the audience, translates the monks' answer as "Any time your mind moves. *Karma* is any time your mind moves."

"How often does your mind move?" he asks us.

We don't answer.

He points to the monks. "I'll ask them."

He claps his hands, smirks, shouts in Tibetan.

The young monks shout back, and Roach tells us they have answered correctly.

"There is a thing called an instant in Tibetan, and it is that long." Roach snaps his fingers to demonstrate the length of an instant. "And in that instant, there are sixty-four subinstants. In that amount of time"—he snaps his fingers again—"your mind moves sixty-four times. And each one of those sixty-four movements is one *karma*." He snaps his fingers. "There goes sixty-four *karmas*." He snaps again. "Another sixty-four." Snap. Snap. "A couple hundred already."

He is working the crowd expertly. We are in the palm of his hand.

"Is that the only kind of *karma*?" he asks us, rhetorically. "Let's check it out!"

Roach and his monk friends shout back and forth. He claps with each question. Swings his *mala*. The young Tibetans frantically shout back answers. The more he claps, the more they shout, trying hard to give him the correct answer.

Finally, Roach grins wide as a Chinese restaurant Buddha, winks at the audience, and we all shout along:

"*Dooooooooooh-chett!*"

According to Roach, the dumb answer was that they failed to identify fully the other sorts of *karma*. I can't either, but I am learning.

Roach tells us that the monks correctly identified a second sort of *karma*—anything you say, and anything you do—mental *karma* and the resultant action or utterance. "And I said, Are those the only kinds of *karma*, and they said, Yeah, and I said, No it isn't."

What they left out, Roach tells us, was good *karma* and bad *karma*. He asks them to define good and bad *karma* for us, and amidst the clapping and shouting, they are successful.

He translates:

"The definition of good *karma* is very interesting. It's not what somebody said to do, it's not what somebody else thinks is right, it's not some guy standing up in the sky somewhere saying that was good or that was bad, it's not what makes you feel good at the moment or what makes you feel bad at the moment. Good *karma* is defined as any thought, word, or action that you do that ultimately brings you some sort of happiness. That is the definition of good *karma*. The definition of bad *karma* is anything you do or think or say that ultimately brings you some sort of pain or suffering."

He asks the monks where *karma* is planted. The audience is transfixed by all the clapping, shouting, *mala*-waving, and wild gesticulating, partly because of Roach's high energy, partly because we are clueless as to what is being said and must wait for an explanation.

Roach turns to us again, grins. "They are much better than last year."

Karma stays in your mind, he explains, in the stream of your mind. He engages the monks in a discussion of whether bad actions can ever create good *karma* or vice versa. He gives them an example, and then explains it to us.

"I'm in the diamond business, part-time," he says, and people laugh, because it seems a silly notion. The man is a Tibetan monk, not a merchant. "My boss is always saying to me, 'There is a guy out there selling diamonds, and those diamonds are worth a thousand dollars a carat, but you go out there and tell him it is worth nine hundred, and stick to it, stick to it for about half an hour, and if he doesn't give up, give him nine fifty, and we'll make fifty dollars.' What did he send me out to do? To lie. But as a result of the lie, I make fifty bucks. Is the profit a nice thing?" he asks.

"It is a nice thing, I mean, who can complain about fifty dollars? And since it is nice, it must have come from what kind of *karma*? It must have come from a good *karma*."

He asks the monks.

They say "no connection."

"Well let's check this out," Roach suggests. "We just happen to have Vanna White here."

Two young women, American students not in monastic robes, unfurl a large white poster with two circle-faces, connected by an arrow. In the top circle, the cartoon face is frowning.

Roach points to the unhappy face. "Michael Roach lies at work," he narrates. He points to the smiling circle face. "Michael Roach has fifty dollars." He pulls out a can of spray paint. "But there is no connection."

With red paint, Roach draws new arrows to new faces, one smiling, one frowning. Now the happy face is connected with another happy face.

"Michael Roach had the happy result of the money because of something good he had done in the past. The result of the bad action, the bad *karma,* is that no one believes you, you become known as a liar. You do not get good things by doing bad things. It totally does not work, according to the laws of *karma.*

"If you want to reach Buddha paradise, you have to be kind to other people. That is the only way to reach Buddha paradise."

ROACH DOESN'T BRING it up, but what he is saying sounds oddly familiar—"For whatsoever a man soweth, that also shall he reap."

It turns out that Roach actually is a diamond merchant, directing a large Manhattan diamond firm. I only discover this later, when I read some of the literature his students have passed around. I am truly dumbfounded, had assumed his example was meant to be absurd. Like Father Kennedy, Roach seems to hold down at least three full-time jobs. When do these people sleep?

ROACH IS WINDING up his act. The banner gets folded, the spray paint put away.

"It is traditional in the last moments of a debate," he says, "to ask a very special question: 'Is it possible for every living creature in the universe to become a fully enlightened Buddha?' I will ask them."

He turns to the young monks and the laughing, enthusiastic crowd grows silent, almost as if we sense that the monks' answer will determine if we ourselves, the sunbathers, in-line skaters, weekend Zen wannabes, and Buddhist investment bankers, can ever become Buddhas.

The students seem to think a moment. Then they grumble something in Tibetan.

Roach claps and shouts, turns to the audience.

"They said yes."

8

THE WORK KOAN

....

Life Without a Cushion

PERHAPS IT is possible for every living creature in the universe to become a fully enlightened Buddha, but in the meantime we have to come up with our rent money and pay our phone bills.

Compassion, enlightenment, mindfulness, karma—these are all wonderful gifts, perhaps—but except for those members of the Rockefeller and Luce family who practice Buddhism, not many of us can, in reality, just sit on a cushion and breathe.

We have to eat, for instance.

Buddhist monks of old solved this problem by wandering from village to village, begging for rice. Today, though, even monks must hold jobs—operating snazzy retreat centers, traveling the lecture circuit, selling diamonds—and of course, most of us aren't monks.

I have mentioned *koans*, the unanswerable Zen riddles that seem designed to confound beginning students. Perhaps the most difficult *koan* in current Buddhist practice, it occurs to me, especially for lay Buddhists, is how to make a living without turning your back on

everything you believe. All that goofiness in Central Park was good
fun, but if I am going to be a Buddhist, and stay married, hold my
job, walk with two feet on the ground, how do I do it?

DEEP IN NORTH Carolina's Great Smoky Mountains, a location so
lush and magnificent it would threaten to make a Buddhist out of
anyone, Linsi Deyo wrestles with just this question.

On a Sunday morning, I visit Linsi and her husband, Patrick
Clark, in Cullowhee, and we hike one of the mountains surrounding
their small farm.

The trillium is in bloom, the trees are flowering, the air is soft,
warm, and clear, and it is a perfect day to stroll through nature, except Patrick's idea of relaxation is to hike straight up Rocky Face
Mountain, which seems like a seventy-five-degree incline of thick
bramble, interrupted only by beds of poison ivy. Patrick grew up
here, and I guess he is used to it.

Despite the cool weather, we are all three covered with perspira-
tion by the time we hack through the thickets back down to the couple's metal-roofed house. Patrick, a seemingly inexhaustible packet
of energy, goes off to work on his mandala garden, while Linsi and I
talk and recover.

We sit in her austere office, on old yard-sale chairs, surrounded
by orange crates serving as office furniture. The computer is a prim-
itive Apple. The walls are bare wood, ancient tongue-in-groove pan-
eling. The window frames are warping.

Out of this office, a front room of their rented home, Linsi runs
what she estimates to be the fifth largest *zafu* manufacturing company in the United States. "DharmaCrafts is probably the biggest,"
she guesses, "then Mighty Cushion out of Karme Choling, Shasta
Abbey in California, Zen Home Stitchery, and then I think it is us."

She does some wholesale business, selling her meditation cushions to *dharma* groups, Zen centers, and metaphysical and New Age bookstores, and also a fair bit of individual mail order. Her company, Carolina Morning Designs, also sells books and brass bells of mindfulness, but doesn't really make money on those.

It is a home business in every sense of the word. Linsi sews in the bedroom, Patrick fills orders on the porch, packing materials and supplies are stored in just about every corner of every room, and a UPS rate schedule card is posted at the front door.

LINSI IS FORTY-SEVEN, with shoulder-length graying hair, blue-green eyes, and angular features. She is quick to laugh, but there is also a certain sadness about her, or maybe she is just tired from working so hard.

She was living in Boston in 1980, in a relationship she terms "crummy," working in an office on Boylston Street, about four doors down from the Dharmadatu Center, and one day she went in to check it out, "to see if the meditation would be good for me. And it was!" She sips a cup of tea and thinks back. "I had fantasies about what it would be like to be a Buddhist. I saw these people studying in the Tibetan tradition, and I wanted to be an advanced student too, to take the higher teachings. So I moved into a *sangha* house with about four other students, and I lived there a couple of years."

"How was that?" I ask.

"It was a lesson in illusion. You know, one of many in the continuous lessons in illusion," she laughs. "They were ordinary people, with ordinary problems."

At the same time, Linsi was going to fashion design school, "because I thought I was going to start my own little fashion business out in the boonies." Since she was familiar with sewing, someone at the Dharmadatu Center put her to work in their meditation cushion company. Soon thereafter, she was checking *zafu* quality for Dharma-

Crafts, and also began sewing some cushions on her own, for a small meditation group. She moved to North Carolina a few years later, and worked on staff at the Southern Dharma Retreat Center.

"They were trying to figure out a little cottage industry to help support the center," Linsi explains, "and I suggested maybe we could make cushions. I spent quite a bit of time looking into what it would take to start a business and I presented it all to the board—you know, 'It would cost this much for materials, et cetera, et cetera'—and finally we decided that it wasn't realistic for the center to do it, but they suggested that I consider starting the business myself."

So, she did.

In May 1985, with about $1,500 loaned from her mother, Linsi purchased a Bernina sewing machine and five bolts of cotton/polyester fabric. Slowly but surely, people began to order Carolina Morning Designs cushions. The first year, Linsi sold almost nothing, but in the second she recorded $16,000 in gross sales. Ten years later, that figure has jumped to $53,000, and it continues to grow.

THIS WOULD BE a nice American success story, except Linsi and Patrick are struggling to make ends meet, and she is full of doubts about whether her company is even worth continuing.

Running a Buddhist business is difficult, and Linsi has complications of her own.

Like so many American Buddhists, Linsi is reacting *against* her religious and family upbringing as much as she is embracing a new path. What comes before, it seems, colors everything that comes after.

Linsi was raised in the Finger Lakes region of New York State, and her parents were Baptist and Presbyterian. "I went to church every Sunday with my mother," she says. "When I was growing up, people from the church brought us used clothing and sometimes on the holidays they would bring us food. I was one of five kids. We always had enough to eat, but we were at the edge. I was in school with the doctor's and dentist's kids, so when we went to church in our old car, I would slink down in the backseat."

Some people, brought up in poverty, are drawn to money, to the idea of comfort, security, and wealth, and seek it the rest of their lives. For Linsi it went the other way.

"I realize now how much negativity was placed on people who did have money," she says. "People who had money or people who were successful were considered to have big egos. It was a subtle conditioning I got mainly from my mother."

She traces part of the "people with money are bad" attitude to her mother's religious beliefs. Later, a lesson she learned from her father complicated Linsi's view of money even more.

"By the time I got to high school, my father had found a stable job, for Kodak. He drove an hour into the city and worked the trick shift. He did this for years, and one time in high school, Kodak had a tour for the families.

"I went on that tour and was appalled. It was this barren waste-land where they made film canisters. There would be one person in this hellhole running this gigantic machine, and even though the Kodak people were obviously proud of their factory, I was like, 'He works here?'

"Later on, when I was in college, I came home one day to visit, and I was sitting with my father at the kitchen table, and I said, 'You know, you're an intelligent man, why do you do that? Don't you have any dreams?' I look back now and realize it was really condescend-ing." She stops to think a moment. "At the time, I thought I was being authentic.

"My Dad said 'You wanna know why I work at Kodak?' and he

pushed his paycheck at me, and that made a huge impression. I'm sure I made some crass remark, and immediately in my own mind, I said, 'I'll never sell my soul to do that.' I was being an uppity twenty-year-old, but it tied in with all my money issues."

She started her own business, Linsi theorizes, as a way to avoid the trap she saw her father falling into, a way to be her own boss, set her own hours, a way to "be authentic" and avoid the "hellhole" of factory work and corporate greed.

By one measure—that of sheer volume—she has been successful, but by another—profitability—she has not. "This is a business where the cost of making the product is very high compared to the going market price. There is very, very little markup."

Carolina Morning Designs did manage to gross $53,000 in 1995, but out of that came materials, advertising, shipping, and salaries. In addition to Patrick, she employs three people on a part-time basis to help with sewing and stuffing. In their biggest year, the couple netted a little over $10,000.

"After self-employment taxes, that came out to around eighty-five hundred dollars," she stresses, "for *two* people. So you can see, we live very modestly."

They do.

Patrick grows much of their food, they forgo nearly all luxuries, and just about everything they own is purchased second-hand. Living simply can be romantic, but it is also tough. They have no savings, no health insurance, no cushion of their own.

"It is not pleasant," Linsi says. "There are certain anxieties about not being able to buy some basic things. For example, I can't afford to go to retreats." She laughs and shakes her head. "Do I really have a successful Buddhist business here, when I can't even afford to go to a Buddhist retreat?"

ALL THE TIME we are talking, I watch through the front window as Patrick goes back and forth, back and forth, with his wheelbarrow. He is building a compost pile, recycling old manure from the barn for use in his garden project.

Patrick, at thirty-two, is considerably younger than his wife. He is small, intense, with the taut muscles of a devoted cyclist. He grew up in Cullowhee, in the house right next door, in fact, to the one he and Linsi now rent.

"My orientation to life is pretty Buddhist," he tells me, "but I've never taken any vows, or even studied Buddhism a whole lot."

He started out with Transcendental Meditation—a nonreligious technique based more on Hinduism than Buddhism. "In TM, you pretty much sit in a chair. When I first met Linsi, she was selling these cushions, and I thought they were silly. I'm not going to sit on one of them, I'll fall over! But one day I decided to try it, and I sat on a cushion, and it was pretty comfortable."

Patrick is working as we talk, opening a box of multicolored beach balls. Carolina Morning Designs uses the inflatable balls as the core of their portable *zafu*, "Great for meditators on the go."

A rooster crows next door, and Patrick traces for me his lifelong interest in a philosophy known as "self-propulsion."

"I grew up poor, and I never got a car when I was a teenager, and so I've always been self-propelled, I've always had to walk or bike wherever I've gone. And then one day I got a car and started driving everywhere and I didn't particularly like it—it was sort of unnerving."

He moved to a "land trust" alternative community, "and I realized it felt really good to be in one neighborhood all the time, to be in one place. There was that, and of course the pollution bothered me. That was the point that I realized that I had a certain lifestyle—I had already been into it—but that was when the bell rang and said 'Oh

yeah, I walk, I ride a bike, and there is no reason to be ashamed of it.'
A car is in many ways just a vehicle to hold our ego."

"We need cars to get to our jobs," I say, "because we need the job
to pay for the car."

"Right, right."

Cars, with their air conditioning, windows, sound systems, and
great speed, keep us isolated from our environment, Patrick explains, whereas "self-propulsion," such as biking, walking, canoeing,
puts us in touch with the land below us and the world around us.
It's healthier, Patrick asserts, for the environment certainly, but for
people as well.

For a while, he and Linsi edited a magazine, *Kokopelli Notes*, es-
pousing the self-propelled lifestyle, and though they didn't manage
to make any money from that endeavor either, the magazine won a
devoted following and a few national awards.

THEY HAVE BEEN married two years, and just moved back to Cullowhee the previous autumn. Almost right away, Patrick started his
garden.

"I studied permaculture," he explains. "They say that when you
approach a new design for a piece of land, when you design the land
to produce food and meet your basic needs, the best way is to just
kind of get a feel for the land, being on it and kind of letting it speak
to you. Linsi helped me—we walked around and discussed it—it
was just a big square field, and we were thinking of a big square garden with square beds, and then all of a sudden we thought, 'Hey,
let's do a circle!' You can walk around it, you can get from one end to
the next more easily."

We are on the farmhouse's front porch. The garden, in the circular
shape of a Buddhist mandala, is across the road. He has planted
tomatoes, peppers, lettuce, chard, spinach, beans, peas, gourds, and

corn. Cardinals are trilling, kingfishers are flitting from tree to tree, three hawks are circling high overhead, and I point out the obvious: "The garden is beautiful."

Patrick agrees, and his excitement is infectious. The circular design of the garden has its practical aspects—the circle is divided into four quadrants, making it easy to rotate crops, and the various spokes of the mandala make it easy to access any corner. But he is equally excited by the aesthetic aspects. "The effect of being in it, just standing in it or walking in it, is very powerful. It almost seems refreshing, like on the edge of a lake or on the ocean shore."

Patrick is full of projects, ideas, and ideals. He is planning a gazebo for the center of the mandala garden. The gazebo will have a wooden shake roof, walls of natural vines, and a frame of pine—logs from trees planted next door, thirty years earlier, by his brother Victor.

He may grow his own wheat. He wants to terrace the hillside, and plant trees to hide the road. He imagines, someday, running a school for sustainable living—a philosophy that asserts you can live with the land, from it, without despoiling it, without running down the natural resources.

And he hopes eventually to reconstruct a nineteenth-century Appalachian farmstead on the site, right down to the log cabins.

ALREADY, THE NEIGHBORS have made a few comments.

The little hollow where Linsi and Patrick live is very rural, very traditional, and even the simple idea of a round garden is considered weird. "They stop at the fence and make jokes," Patrick admits, "about alien crop circles."

He doesn't seem to mind the neighbors' kidding, though, and in fact brings a certain missionary zeal to his work. "I'm a pioneer of sorts," he tells me, still unpacking the inflatable beach balls. "I'm moving in here, and I'm going to influence this place, influence it the way I want to see the world going to go. I'm just going to be who I am and move up here and, very gently and carefully, do what I need to do. I'm not trying to make any sort of statement about what other people need to do—I'm just trying to set an example on the land of how people can live in a sustainable way."

When I ask him about the *zafu* business, he seems ambivalent.

"There are too many parts to it," he complains, "the ordering, the supplies, the production, the marketing, handling the credit cards. There are just too many parts, and it doesn't work, so we think it is time to think of something else, but every time we think of something else, it has problems too. Everything has its hang-ups."

Clearly, Patrick would prefer being across the road, making things with his hands, moving dirt around, rather than running a mail-order business. But he needs money, and he knows it. His sustainable living projects, even the ideal of living with and from the land, need capital; even if he grows his own food, fells his own trees, he still needs to go to a hardware store for tools, and nails.

He shakes his head, perplexed and frustrated, just like all of us.

"This whole thing about money is just a struggle," he says.

LINSI AND PATRICK aren't the only two people in America wrestling with the money thing. Buddhists, Quakers, serious Catholics, devout Jews—anyone who adheres to the Golden Rule has a certain problem. It is hard to love your fellow man and still make a killing in the marketplace.

But some are finding ways.

Up in Vermont, Ben and Jerry bring Buddhist principles into their ice cream business, donating some of their profit to progressive causes, and capturing a large portion of the high-end frozen treat market. Too much Monkey Mind? Have a Peace Pop!

Buddhist journals are filled with ads for right livelihood enterprises, some in areas you might expect—health food, natural fiber clothing—and others in areas not quite so New Agey. Along with *dharma* dentists, there are hundreds of Buddhist counselors and psychotherapists practicing across the country. In Cambridge, Massachusetts, George D. Kinder, a bright-eyed financial planner, leads Buddhist retreats as well as seminars on investment and asset management, allowing us to get our lives and our portfolios in order at the same time.

One of the best-known Buddhist livelihood projects is run by Zen monk Bernard Tetsugen Glassman, *sensei* to Father Kennedy and Helen Tworkov. A former systems engineer for McDonnell Douglas, Glassman taught meditation classes to executives there while at the same time working on a flight plan to Mars.

He quit that in 1976, though, and started his own Zen community, in Yonkers, New York, just north of Manhattan. He operates housing for the homeless, a youth center with counseling services, and a daycare facility for low-income Yonkers parents. To help fund all of this, he also operates Greyston Bakery, making gourmet cookies, brownies, cakes, and pies, for Balducci's, Macy's department store, and Ben and Jerry's Homemade, Inc. The bakery does over $1.5 million in annual sales.

"You can't define Zen any more than you can define life itself," Glassman writes in his book, *Instructions to the Cook: A Zen Master's Lesson for Living a Life that Matters.* "When people visit our community, and they see the bakery and the social action work, somebody always asks, 'Yes, but is it Zen?'"

"It is," Glassman answers. Unlike other philanthropist entrepreneurs, Glassman does not consider his bakery to be simply a way of supporting Zen compassion, he considers the bakery to be Zen itself.

You can meditate mindfully, he points out, or you can make cookies mindfully. Same thing, either way.

LINSI DEYO BELIEVES she is doing some good with Carolina Morning Designs, helping to encourage people everywhere to meditate, to look into their lives more closely and make better choices. Just as she and Patrick try to integrate their spiritual beliefs with their garden, with the land they live on, with their commitment to self-propelled transportation, she tries to run the business fairly and compassionately. As Geshe-la said, we seek enlightenment for the benefit of others.

But she isn't sure how much longer the *zafu* company will continue to exist. As her cat, Solar, weaves around our feet, she begins to tie her long story together.

"Patrick and I don't know if we are going to go on with this," she says. "There is this desire, you know, to feel comfortable. We don't make enough money to do the things we need to do. So that sort of fits with the question, 'Can I let myself make money? Do I still hold that conditioning that being successful is bad?'

"It's sort of ironic that I have all of these issues with money, and here I am operating a meditation-related business. A lot of Buddhists have tremendous issues around money, and a lot of the people who sell my cushions, if they are related to Buddhist centers, they themselves don't want to make any money off the cushions—it's like it's tainted money."

Linsi had to raise her prices the previous year, in response to the cost of raw materials going up, but found to her amazement that one of her regular customers, a meditation teacher, kept selling at the old price, which was now *below* wholesale, thus taking a small loss.

"The Buddha said that having money wasn't bad, it was just clinging to it that was bad," Linsi says, shaking her head. "The Buddha never said you had to live in poverty."

THE DESIRE FOR things, the clinging and dissatisfaction that the Buddha called *dukkha,* is a form of suffering, but so is the constant struggle to survive, the constant worry of paying bills, meeting payroll, staying afloat.

Linsi, it seems, is locked into her own personal cycle of *samsara,* her own circular *koan.*

"Is it possible to make money in this business? And if it is possible, can I let myself do it?" she asks. "If I was making money—let's say Patrick and I were making forty thousand a year—would I be a shame to the Buddhist community?

"And if it isn't possible to make money in this business, can I let myself make money some other way?"

The Buddha also preaches compassion, and though Linsi seems to have compassion for just about everyone, she is just starting to realize that perhaps she has been leaving one person out.

"Can I find a place where I can be compassionate to myself?" she wonders. "Can I find a way to be a little compassionate, and let myself have some money?"

9

THE PLAIN-SPOKEN
THERAVADAN

....

A High View from a Low Seat

BY THIS TIME, my Buddhist experience has run from the sublime to the ridiculous, and some basic questions remain unanswered—Can I actually do it? Can the Catholic kid from Good Shepherd become, if not enlightened, then at least more mindful, less simian, less prone to the mental formations that create *dukkha,* a Buddhist umbrella term meaning dissatisfaction, angst, the self-created cycle of suffering—pretty much defining the rock that Brother Damien thought was my faith?

Those questions, though, turn into circular distractions—thinking about whether I am really up to the task makes me tense, and being tense makes it hard for me to meditate, which makes me doubt myself all the more. So I escape back to my Project Mind, and schedule yet another retreat, this time at a Theravada monastery in High View, West Virginia.

Theravada is a branch of the very oldest form of Buddhism—Hinayana—tracing itself back to the times and language of the original Shakyamuni Buddha. I'm not sure, though, if I am drawn to High View for this reason, or because the name of the town amuses me.

DRIVING THERE A few weeks later, I pass auto graveyards, gunsmithing shops, tumbledown log cabins, and loads of rusting farm machinery. I am south of the Mason-Dixon line—there is a Civil War battlefield just a few miles across the Virginia border—and there is no denying that this corner of West Virginia is rural, definitely chainsaw country.

In High View itself, which turns out to be little more than a few houses along a two-lane road, I stop at Mac's Chicken Shack to ask directions. A curly-haired woman at the cash register seems startled when I walk through the door, which I interpret to mean that business has been slow.

The woman is cashier, cook, and waitress, all rolled up into one. Mac's Chicken Shack is nothing more than a single-room cinderblock building—a garage, really—set next to what is probably the woman's home. I'm laying odds that Mac is her husband.

"Is there a Buddhist monastery near here?" I ask.

The woman gives me a long blank look, which is more or less what I had expected.

"Oh well," I answer, and buy a small bottle of spring water from a stand-up cooler. There is no smell of food in the room. I doubt she has had a customer for hours, perhaps not all day.

As I pay for my drink, though, something seems to click in the woman's brain, and she asks, "Do you mean the Bhavana people?"

"The Bhavana Society," I agree.

The woman's four-year-old daughter is behind me, wiping down the restaurant's three tables and busily talking to no one. I can't hear what she is saying, but she has been happily yammering since I first walked in the door.

"She likes to chat," the woman explains.

I turn to the young girl. "Hello, there. The tables sure look nice."
She beams a jumbo smile back at me.

Good *karma.*

"The Bhavana is about a mile off," the girl's mother says. She gives
me directions—there are only a few turns, watch for the cemetery.
She seems particularly pleased to reassure me that the roads are
"hard surface all the way."

OFF THE HIGHWAY and onto Back Creek Road, the area seems even
more rural, further isolated. The houses are set way back in the
woods. Most of the driveways have gates, and most of the gates are
closed. The Bhavana Society has no gate, and its driveway is marked
by a small wooden sign. In a moment I am parked in a dirt lot. When
I start up the gravel driveway on foot, a gray Mazda truck bears
down on me. Behind the wheel, a man in an orange watch cap lifts a
hand in greeting.

It is not until he pulls up directly next to me and I am staring into
the cab that I see the orange robes under his brown jacket. "They call
me Bhante Dhamma," he says in slow, measured speech. "Bhante" is
a simple title, like "Reverend." "Have you been here before?"

"No," I answer.

"Oh." He seems to think about this awhile, as if this new information demanded some painstaking analysis, then points me toward
the men's dorm. Before I go, though, he explains slowly and carefully
that there is usually a sign near the front door of the men's quarters
reading PLEASE REMOVE YOUR SHOES, but the sign has fallen down
because the tape holding it up has worn out. Would I ever be willing
to tape it back up where it belongs since I was going that way anyway, if it was not too much trouble? It seems an elaborate way to ask
for such a modest favor, but he seems sincere. He smiles, then hands
me some masking tape.

"The sign is probably on the floor," he explains. "Oh, and we have a dog. His name is Brown. He might start nipping at your feet, but he won't hurt you. If he's a bother, just throw a stick into the woods to distract him. He'll chase it down."

The lanky, soft-spoken monk drives off in his little truck, and I keep walking. The dog, a half-collie, finds me and sniffs my ankles but doesn't seem much interested.

The dorm is an old one-story house with three bedrooms, probably someone's hunting cabin years back, before the Buddhists bought it. After I've taped up the sign, I choose a room with two bunk beds, spend about five minutes stowing my gear and fixing up my bunk, then head outside.

Bhante Dhamma has returned and is waiting for me. The back of his Mazda truck is piled high with large sections of wallboard.

"You wouldn't ever be able to help me unload some of this, would you?" he inquires.

Of course, who wouldn't? But he takes none of this for granted. He is open to any possibility. I might say yes, I might say no. I might turn blue and float into the sky.

"Oh, that's really good of you," he says, when I offer a hand.

One at a time, we maneuver six large rectangles of wallboard into the basement of the building, stacking them up against some lumber. The Bhavana Society is undergoing an expansion: a newer, nicer meditation hall is being built—slowly, as funds come in.

Bhante Dhamma drives off on another chore, and I walk back downhill. In addition to the men's dorm, there is a larger main building, which houses the kitchen, the women's dorm, and the meditation hall. There are also a dozen or so *kutis* scattered about through the woods—tiny one-room cabins, like overgrown playhouses, each with a front door, two side windows, and a pipe chimney. The monks and nuns each have their own *kuti*, and some of the weekend guests use them as well.

On first impression, the Bhavana Society grounds and buildings are a disappointment to me. My mind, despite Geshe-la's advice, still forms mental attachments and preconceptions. Knowing I would be in a place called High View, I expected to be atop a mountain, with a view, and lush, verdant vegetation, perhaps a hidden Shangri-La. Instead, I find myself in a scrubby construction site, a valley dominated by felled trees and muddy tire ruts.

I SETTLE IN on a bench in the main building and watch the other participants arrive in clumps and bunches. Before long there are twenty of us, clutching teacups and looking expectant: regular folks of all ages, sizes, shapes, and ethnicities. The side walls of the meditation hall are stacked with cushions; we choose our own and set them in the middle of the floor.

The first meditation session of the retreat lasts about thirty minutes, then the head monk, Bhante Henepola Gunaratana, opens with a small talk. Everyone calls him Bhante G. A small, bright-eyed man in his late sixties, with skin the color of dark copper, he is founder of the Bhavana Society. He was born in Sri Lanka and has been a Buddhist monk since the age of twelve.

With a few questions, Bhante G. determines that everyone in the room has done meditation before, so he skips over the "how to cross your legs" instruction and moves directly into a discussion of our purpose in meditating, then introduces us to the Eight Precepts, a set of basic Buddhist principles that we are to observe while on the Bhavana grounds.

We repeat after him:

I undertake the training rule to abstain from taking life.
I undertake the training rule to abstain from stealing.
I undertake the training rule to abstain from incelibacy.

I undertake the training rule to abstain from false speech.

I undertake the training rule to abstain from intoxicating drinks and drugs causing heedlessness.

I undertake the training rule to abstain from eating at improper times.

I undertake the training rule to abstain from dancing, singing, music, shows, wearing garlands, using perfumes, and beautifying with cosmetics.

I undertake the training rule to abstain from the use of high and large seats and beds.

These are Theravada vows, similar in some ways to the vows all Buddhist monks take, but with a few variations.

The first two rules seem reasonable, and the third makes sense in context. The fourth and fifth are fine, and the sixth rule—no eating at improper times—I will talk about later.

The seventh precept—no show tunes, no impromptu Hawaiian luaus, no eyeliner—seems a bit austere, but then again this is a silent, spiritual retreat.

The eighth and final precept leaves me clueless.

After Bhante G. finishes his brief remarks, we chant in Pali, an ancient language related to Sanskrit, similar to what the original Buddha spoke. When I say "we" chant in Pali, I mean of course that the four monks and two nuns chant in Pali, and the rest of us make little grunting noises trying to follow along.

A bell is rung, and we are silent again, meditating for about thirty more minutes. Then Bhante Dhamma, my slow-speaking friend with the Mazda truck, lays down a few rules—mostly practicalities about use of the showers, preserving hot water, how the kerosene heaters work for those in the *kutis*. He also warns us that if we want to do any walking meditation outside, we should "stay near the main building."

"The neighbors—" he begins to explain, but then hesitates, seeming to have second thoughts about what he was going to say. "Well, the neighbors aren't hostile, they are . . ."

He doesn't finish the sentence with anything more than a shrug, so in my mind, I finish it for him:

The neighbors are . . . annoyed?

The neighbors are . . . a bit confused?

The neighbors are . . . totally freaked out?

I DOUBT THAT many Buddhist monks were spotted in Hampshire County, West Virginia, before 1988, when the Bhavana Society was established. I doubt, too, that High Viewers saw many Sri Lankans before Bhante Gunaratana arrived, much less Sri Lankans with shaved heads, orange robes, and everpresent beatific smiles.

Indeed, the neighbors, I find out later, *are* hostile, or have been at least. Early in the monastery's history, a local version of the Welcome Wagon came by regularly and shot rifles into the air at night. One evening, Bhante G. bravely ventured out to see what they wanted.

A man confronted the monk, pointed to his robes, and demanded to know, "Hey, why aren't those sheets on your bed?"

When interviewed later by a reporter from a Charleston newspaper, Bhante G. explained that he wasn't really bothered by the question. "It simply showed that they were curious."

BEING OF A less generous nature than Bhante G., I crawl into my bunk that night wondering if our Mountain State neighbors are going to sneak in and murder us all in our sleep.

Perhaps I have seen too many movies.

Perhaps I am sitting on my high seat.

• • •

SATURDAY

I have learned this much—Buddhists wake up early.

At the Bhavana Society, a large metal gong reverberates through the woods at five A.M., and should you somehow manage to snooze through that, the neighborhood dogs immediately explode into a barking frenzy.

I stumble down the hill in the morning darkness to the meditation hall, where we sit on our cushions from five-thirty to six-thirty. I have learned, by the way, to stop my watch from beeping, so that isn't a problem here.

Not able to concentrate in the least, I look around, take stock of the place. The room is large—a careful driver could park an even dozen Volkswagen buses here. At the front, a carved-wood table, with an ornate red-and-gold lacquer design, is topped by a larger-than-life Buddha figure, painted bright gold. Below the large Buddha is a smaller one, in black.

A large banner hangs behind the altar, and another hangs from the ceiling above where we sit. Both banners are covered by large orange, white, yellow, and red squares.

For the first hour, I am a squirming, unsettled mess.

This is going to be a debacle, it occurs to me. I never should have come. I am stuck in this eccentric little monastery in rural West Virginia, forced to be silent, with no place to hide. My Monkey Mind continues its gymnastic romp, but thankfully the time passes, and we move on to walking meditation.

We did walking meditation—Zen Buddhists call it *kinhin*—at Zen Mountain Monastery as well, but here it is much different. On Monkey Mind Mountain, *kinhin* was a vigorous, heart-pumping sprint. We would circle the meditation hall so fast, in fact, that the monastery staff had taped little arrows to the floor, pointing the way, so we wouldn't slam into one another.

At the Bhavana Society, we walk with excruciating slowness: on one prolonged inhalation of breath, we lift one foot; on the exhalation, we move it slightly forward and lower it; on the subsequent inhalation, we lift the other foot; and on the next exhalation, we lower that one.

It takes roughly five full minutes to cross the twenty-five foot width of the meditation hall, and another five to get back. We look like big wading birds poking through a swamp.

And I'm still on my high seat, still thinking about the rural neighbors and what they might think if they snuck up through the woods and looked through the window.

"My Gawd Earlene," I imagine Clem exclaiming. "It's just like that zombie movie."

BREAKFAST IS AT seven. We carry benches in from the hallway, line the walls with them, and then sit behind the benches on the floor, facing into the center of the room.

The monastery cook rings a bell, and Bhante G. rises from his cushion, walks slowly—really slowly—across the meditation hall to the doorway that links us to the kitchen. He is followed by the three other resident monks, each as thin and straight as a buckwheat noodle, walking even more slowly than Bhante G. The monks are followed by the two resident nuns. These other monastics are not Sri Lankan. The men, and one of the women, are American-born; the other nun is German.

As they file toward the kitchen, all seven of the monastics clutch large bowls to their chests. These are the begging bowls once used by monks in Asia who would wander from village to village asking for sustenance. The Bhavana monks don't wander from village to village, but they accept their food only after the cook offers it to them in a ritual that recalls the ancient practice.

When the monks and nuns are seated again with their bowls in front of them, the rest of us are permitted to go for our food. We use plates, not bowls, and help ourselves to the stewed prunes, banana slices, apple slices, hot oatmeal, whole grain cereal, and yogurt. These people must have the world's healthiest bowels, I think to myself.

We eat slowly—the idea is to chew what is in our mouths before we fill our spoons with the next bite. This is not how I eat at home, by the way. Like many, I am prone to shovel my food, a mad race against time, so fast I barely taste it sometimes. I know it isn't healthy, yet can't seem to stop.

Eating slowly, on the other hand, is mindfulness in practice. I am taking a bite of oatmeal, I know that I am taking a bite of oatmeal, I feel the blandness on my tongue, I notice the grainy texture of the fiber-rich oatmeal as I chew, and I feel the thick, gelatinous mass lumping down my throat.

After breakfast, the others scatter about to make their beds or wash their hair, or on various assigned chores, and I do the dishes. Zen Mountain Monastery had an institutional dishwashing machine worthy of a prosperous restaurant. The Bhavana Society has three sinks, one of which leaks, and a bunch of sponges.

At eight-thirty, we are sitting again, alternating an hour on the pillow with a half hour of egret walking. Through the course of the morning, I adjust my sitting position, using two *zafus* instead of the customary one, and I find myself starting to relax.

Before long, I am feeling quite comfortable, the stress draining from my body. Buddhism intends to be much more than a stress relaxation technique, of course, though many Americans are happy enough if that's all they manage, and for the next few hours I am among the easily pleased.

LUNCH IS AT eleven, a vegetable stir-fry and bean soup. Simple but tasty. It will be our last meal of the day (Precept Six.) The Theravada monks here follow this rule every day of the year, and I entered the weekend knowing full well that I would have to conform. So, I load up my plate.

We sit again after lunch, and I am feeling pretty good. I have violated hardly any of the precepts, and though I've only been here about eighteen hours, seven of them asleep, I'm beginning to feel like an old hand. I'm also looking forward to my chance for an interview with Bhante G.

Unlike ZMM's rigid *dokusan* ritual, all I have to do for this interview is sign up on a clipboard, and I do this, taking the first slot, at three P.M.

When my time comes, I walk across the driveway to the small cabin that serves as the head monk's office, and he is waiting for me in a swivel chair. I've noticed some of the weekend participants bowing when they see him, and others not bowing. We have been given no instruction one way or the other, so I just nod and shrug, trying to cover all the bases.

Bhante G. seems nothing more than amused by my awkward entry. He is wearing a red watch cap and an orange jacket over his robes, and since the office is quite chilly, he leaves the extra clothing on. Instead of cushions, we are seated in office chairs, a cluttered desk between us.

He smiles.

I smile back.

He smiles even more.

I smile like a grinning baboon.

Bhante G. rescues me from my own dull-wittedness. "Do you have a question?" he invites.

I had forgotten that I was supposed to ask something. The old copper monk has an amazingly calm presence, and I think that I just wanted to bask in it awhile. It would have been fine with me if no one had said a word for ten minutes. But I finally blurt out, "I'm a beginner"—as if he hadn't noticed—"and I'm having a problem with my wandering mind."

He smiles again, even wider than before, as if my admission has brought him pure joy, as if I've just told him he won the West Virginia lottery. "Oh, you have a wandering mind?"

I nod.

He couldn't be happier. "Ah, this is normal," he advises. "To have a wandering mind is very normal. Yes. Never become discouraged by this."

I nod again.

"Nothing that is good comes easily. Some of what is bad comes easily for us, of course, but none of what is good. Our minds are full of thoughts—" he hesitates only a moment here, framing his next words, then continues "—not just from this lifetime, you see. From our previous lifetimes as well."

Bhante G. laughs. Perhaps the idea of previous lifetimes, and the piles of thought garbage we accumulate, amuses him, or perhaps he is aware that to the Western mind, reincarnation is one of Buddhism's most foreign notions.

"We have all these thoughts, you see, and they do not go away quickly."

I can't argue there.

"Be kind to yourself," he advises further. "Don't ever think, 'Oh, she is meditating so well and I am not,' or 'Look, the one over there is so concentrated.' Perhaps they have thoughts too."

His eyes sparkle a little on the last statement, and it occurs to me that perhaps he is admitting to the occasional stray thought himself. Though he is as placid and serene as a Buddha statue on his *zafu* during our hour-long meditations, perhaps he loses focus, too, and starts to daydream about his Sri Lankan boyhood, or about lunch.

He nods and smiles—my question is answered—but instead of ringing a bell so I can bow madly and scoot away like a Zen cockroach, Bhante G. leans back in his chair. "What do you do?" he asks.

I tell him that I teach writing to college students.

He brightens again and goes to his bookshelf, pulls down a copy of his latest book, *Mindfulness in Plain English,* and hands it to me. He seems very proud as he tells me that it has been translated into German, Italian, Spanish, Russian, French, and Chinese, among others. The book is getting excellent notices here as well, in the United States. We discuss the difficulties of writing clearly, and he expresses mild concern that his editor has moved on to another position at another publishing house, and he will be working with a new editor on his next book.

It is tempting, by the way, to see Bhante Gunaratana as just a simple little man in funny clothes—he has been a monk for nearly fifty years and has presumably, by following the eight precepts, missed out on a lot of what we Westerners might consider to be normal experience. But looks can be deceiving. In addition to writing his books, Bhante G. is an internationally known *dharma* teacher, and has been around the world many times over, lecturing and leading retreats throughout Asia, Europe, in New Zealand, and across America. He has a Ph.D. in philosophy from American University. He is carving a monastery out of thirty-two acres of rough land with very little money. The man has done much more in his life than just sit on a pillow and watch his thoughts.

Bhante G. is so much more approachable and human than John

Daido Loori seemed during my disastrous *dokusan* a few months earlier. We are just two guys chewing the fat, and he doesn't seem at all concerned about the time. I leave after fifteen minutes, only because he has another appointment. I would have loved to talk all day.

THE AFTERNOON CONSISTS of sitting and walking.

You get the picture by now. We sit, we walk, occasionally we eat, when there is a break we sip tea in silence, and not much else happens. Bhante G. gives the occasional instruction, and one of the kitchen helpers speaks to me briefly in order to show me how the dishes should be washed, but other than that, we are left with our thoughts.

The lack of verbal chatter helps to quiet the mind. The monkey in my brain is nowhere near ready to throw in the towel, of course, but he eventually begins to calm down, putting his feet up and surveying the landscape. He continues to comment on what he sees, but with a lessening frequency and intensity.

I imagine my monkey on a front porch somewhere, in a monkey-size rocking chair, watching the sun go down. The little guy has never been so relaxed in his life.

Not that *I* would know, of course, being nowhere near enlightened, but I imagine that maybe enlightenment is when the monkey in that rocker looks out over the mountains, sees the sunset, and doesn't think, "Damn, I need to find a better job," but just sees the sunset.

Moreover, the monkey doesn't even think, "Gee, I love this sunset, I hope it lasts forever." Positive attachments create *dukkha* as well.

Maybe enlightenment is when the monkey just sees the sunset, and then, when the sunset ends, the monkey just looks at the stars.

AS THE WEEKEND proceeds, I am increasingly struck by some practical differences between the two monasteries I have visited. Zen
Mountain Monastery, though I thought it a bit austere at the time,
seems now to be the Club Med of retreat centers, while Bhavana is a
run-down, family-owned and -operated motor inn on a back highway somewhere. I'm not talking about the service, of course—no
one at either place will bring a bucket of ice to your room at two
A.M.—but the facilities.

I am also aware that there is far less rigmarole here at the Bhavana
Society. Though there are some odd rules in the printed material—
never face the soles of your feet in the direction of the monks, for instance—in practice things are quite simple. We basically get seated
on our *zafus* in the morning and just sit there all day. If someone has
to pee, they get up quietly and go pee. If someone comes in late, they
come in late. If you want to bow to a monk, a nun, or a Buddha
statue, go ahead, but no one is keeping track. Squirming around or
switching of leg positions is not encouraged, but it's not really discouraged either. The monks lead by example—Bhante G. never
switches.

So maybe, it occurs to me, I am getting closer to a truer form of
"American" Buddhism, to the goal of my Project. It is tempting to
think so—there is the rural West Virginia setting, for instance, the
piles of freshly chopped firewood everywhere lending a certain pioneer spirit to the grounds, and there is Bhante Dhamma tooling
around in his Mazda truck. Add in the barking dogs, and the simplicity of Bhante G.'s instructions—we have an interview, rather
than *dokusan*—and it starts to seem very homegrown.

But of course, the Bhavana retreat is brimming with Sri Lankan
overtones, such as the decor of the altar, the food, the various chants
and invocations in Pali, just as Zen Mountain Monastery reflected

the Japanese origins of its brand of Zen, and just as Geshe-la's retreat was a taste of Tibet.

So what, then, will American Buddhism really look like?

Blue denim robes? Broccoli and cheese casserole, instead of stir-fry and rice?

Perhaps someday we will sit on our plastic *zafus*, in our Gap robes, chanting, "Um, the Buddha is pretty cool. Um, the Buddha taught us the Four Nifty Truths. Um, we will try to do what he said."

Silly thoughts, but I amuse myself with them.

WHEN WE WOULD normally be eating dinner, had we not promised to forego all food after the early lunch, we have yoga. The monk Bhante Yogavacara Rahula is our instructor, and though he has seemed severe and intimidating up until now—he is gaunt, silent, and tends to scowl as he sits on his cushion—he turns out to be quite warm and friendly.

He is American, and his story is interesting. Born Scott DuPrez, in California, he spent time in Vietnam as a reluctant American soldier, then did the sixties hippie thing, wandering across Europe and Asia, was once busted in Afghanistan on drug charges, and eventually ended up in India, then Sri Lanka, where he became a Buddhist. He is now the second-ranking monk, seated to Bhante G.'s left, and well known himself in Buddhist circles. He, too, travels internationally to teach the *dharma* and lead retreats.

We stretch, extend our arms, legs, tongues, roll our eyes, arch our backs, and after a day of sitting, it feels wonderful. "Notice how the exercise makes you feel," he reminds us again and again. "Where do you feel a warmth, a tingling?"

By the end of the thirty-minute yoga class, I feel warm and tingly virtually all across my sedentary, middle-aged, overweight body, and it is a fantastic sensation.

AFTERWARD, OF COURSE, we sit meditation some more, drink gallons of tea, and finish with a talk from Bhante G.

I am so relaxed, I barely listen, which is not mindful of me, but for once in my life I am not trying to figure things out with my brain, not relying on my verbal skills to excel, not trying to be the best student in the class. I am just sitting on the cushion, feeling rather contented. Progress?

We finish and head for our dorm around nine-thirty P.M.

Though I've skipped dinner and my usual snacks, I'm not hungry. And though no one is checking up on us—the monks and nuns are quite a distance off, nestled in their *kutis* deep in the woods—my three roommates and I continue to observe Noble Silence. One fellow softly asks to borrow my toothpaste, but that is it.

SUNDAY

Sitting. Walking. Sitting. Walking. Breakfast. Sitting. Walking. The routine doesn't change.

During the break after lunch, I retreat to my room to read from Bhante Gunaratana's, *Mindfulness in Plain English*. (In another departure from Zen Mountain Monastery, the Bhavana Society does not have a store, but it does have a book rack, and you can simply help yourself, slipping whatever donation you feel appropriate into a box.)

"Meditation is not easy," he writes. "It takes time and it takes energy. It also takes grit, determination, and discipline. It requires a host of personal qualities which we normally regard as unpleasant and which we like to avoid wherever possible . . . So why bother? Why waste all that time and energy when you could be out enjoying yourself?"

He has a good way of cutting through that tendency of Buddhist teachings to seem like babble, circular *koans* that roll off the tongue, off the mind, and leave one back where one started. This is a problem with Buddhism—everyone insists the experience cannot be put into words, that enlightenment is indescribable. But Bhante Gunaratana seems as clear of pen as he is of mind.

"Why?" he writes. "Simple. Because you are human, you find yourself heir to an inherent unsatisfactoriness in life which simply will not go away. You can suppress it from your awareness for a time. You can distract yourself for hours on end, but it always comes back —usually when you least expect it."

He is right on the money. He is talking about the emptiness inside, the "something missing" feeling that has been there since my first Catholic retreat and before, the "dis-ease" that made me investigate all this Buddha stuff in the first place.

"So what is wrong with you?" Bhante G. asks. "Are you a freak? No. You are just human. And you suffer from the same malady that infects every human being. It is a monster inside all of us, and it has many arms: chronic tension, lack of genuine compassion for others, including the people closest to you, feelings being blocked up, and emotional deadness. Many, many arms. None of us is entirely free from it. We may deny it. We try to suppress it. We build a whole culture around hiding from it, pretending it is not there, and distracting ourselves from it with goals and projects and status. But it never goes away. It is a constant undercurrent in every thought and every perception; a little wordless voice at the back of the head that keeps saying, 'Not good enough yet. Got to have more. Got to make it better. Got to be better.'"

You would think he grew up somewhere in Ohio, and went to Catholic school. He is describing, it seems to me, the essential American character.

"Life seems to be a perpetual struggle, some enormous effort against staggering odds. And what is our solution to all this dissatisfaction? We get stuck in the 'if only' syndrome. If only I had more money, then I would be happy. If only I could find somebody who would really love me, if only I could lose twenty pounds, if only I had a color TV, a Jacuzzi, and curly hair, and on and on forever.

"So where does all this junk come from, and more important, what can we do about it? It comes from the conditions of our own minds. It is a deep, subtle, and pervasive set of mental habits, a Gordian knot which we have built up bit by bit and we can unravel just that same way, one piece at a time. We can tune up our awareness, dredge up each separate piece, and bring it out into the light. We can make the unconscious conscious, slowly, one piece at a time."

That is the essence of meditation, he writes: insight. Bringing the unconscious mental habits that send us spinning into frenzies of thought and worry into the light, where we can be free of them.

WE HAVE LUNCH. More sitting. More slow walking. Sitting. Walking. Sitting. Walking. Sitting. Yoga. More sitting.

By the end of the second full day, I feel light as a small ball of cotton. All of the deep breathing has brought oxygen to corners of my brain and bloodflow to places in my body I had forgotten existed. ("Call the deprogrammers, Earlene. There's another one hooked.") My body is so imbued with what Bhante Rahula calls *prajna* energy that I find myself stopping in the hallway outside the meditation room and staring through the trees off into the distance, to see my little blue car in the parking lot, just to reassure myself that it is still there, that the outside world is still there, that I am still the encumbered, muddled fellow who arrived two days earlier.

Late Sunday night at the final *dharma* talk, I feel truly blissful, and though I am leaving in the morning and part of me is, as always, anxious to hit the road, another part of me really wants to stay. My legs no longer ache, and with the new configurations of pillows and mats, I feel as if I could sit forever.

When he is done teaching that evening, Bhante G. asks, "Any questions?"

He waits, while the students sit on their cushions and think. No one volunteers.

When he realizes we have nothing to ask of him, he raises his right hand, and with a big smile and bright eyes, joins his thumb and forefinger into a circle, and seems to wink at us.

Everything is A-OK!

MONDAY

I leave at dawn, the sun just breaking through the West Virginia clouds, the lights just starting to switch on in the trailers, the rough, sheet-metal shacks, and the occasional ranch house. Some of the retreat participants will be staying on through the week, and I envy them.

This retreat was quite an experience, a powerful experience, really, though it embarrasses me to say so, because I have been trained to scoff at such seemingly mystical episodes.

Indeed, I have already encountered the scorn of my fellow cynics. "You aren't becoming a Buddhist, are you?" my sister-in-law asked me. "You don't think there's anything to that stuff?" inquired a fellow at work. These remarks were prompted simply by the news that I was to attend the retreat. If I told my friends and colleagues that I was not only attending, the reporter secretly taking notes in the men's room, but buying into it, feeling real spiritual change, I would probably find myself dropped from a number of invitation lists.

TRAVELING NORTH THROUGH West Virginia, then Virginia, then Maryland, I feel content, recharged.

When I reach Pennsylvania, I detour onto a two-lane highway, and for a full hour traveling up and down a set of eroded mountains I am stuck behind the same truck. It is a big white tractor-trailer, and on the backdoors, in green block letters, it says BE KIND, BE CAREFUL, BE YOURSELF.

I smile.

The Buddha's teachings are everywhere.

10

BUDDHA BUG, BUDDHA BEING

You Are What You Eat

I SET THEM free on a chilly morning in mid-May.

They were sleepy, clinging to the inside of the cotton bag, and at first I wasn't quite sure how to get them out. I could reach in and scoop with my hand, but I imagined crushing some between my fingers, generating innumerable negative *karmas*. I could turn the bag over and shake, but I wasn't sure how far they could fall without being injured. So eventually, I just hung the cloth bag from the new foliage of a Carefree Wonder rosebush and let them find their own way out.

With the morning sun warming the dew, the ladybugs began to swarm from the bag like creatures from a B movie. They seemed a bit stunned by the transition, moving in slow motion, some wobbling and falling, and seemingly not able to get righted. I found myself trying to turn them over with a twig, to get them on their little black legs again, which wasn't easy, and probably wasn't smart. God knows what the neighbors thought.

Ladybugs, especially sleepy, refrigerated ladybugs, tend to trudge along as if doing walking meditation, the slow Theravada sort of walking meditation—and there were approximately 4,500 mail-order ladybugs balled up inside the cloth bag. My act of insect emancipation was taking forever.

I watched until I couldn't stand the wait any longer, then just left the bag hanging off the branch and went inside to work on my computer. When I sat down, I discovered that one of the ladybugs had come inside on my shirtsleeve. I named him Sid—short for Siddhartha—lifted him onto my desk, and he crawled happily around the outer edge of my computer monitor for a good while, as I wrote this account.

WHEN THE BUDDHA set down his precepts, a set of rules that closely resemble the Judeo-Christian Ten Commandments, his first precept was "Do not kill; refrain from the taking of life."

While Christians have by and large interpreted their own First Commandment to mean "Do not kill other human beings" (and of course, throughout history there have been horrible exceptions allowed even to this narrow interpretation), Buddhists tend to take a broader view of their rule.

Along with the Ten Cardinal Precepts, the Three Treasures, the Four Noble Truths, and the Eight Gates, the Buddha (a big believer in numbered lists) left his followers the Four Great Vows. The first of these reads, "Sentient beings are numberless; I vow to save them."

Putting this vow to save all sentient beings (sentient means capable of feeling or perception) alongside the precept not to kill and adding in the historical Buddha's teachings on compassion has led Buddhists to value *all* life, be it human, animal, plant, insect, even vermin.

It all comes back to nonduality, a concept that is awfully hard for

Westerners, and perhaps Asians as well, to fully perceive. We are not separate creatures, separate entities, the Buddha taught, we are all one interconnected reality.

Though this has become apparent to many people lately on a practical, ecological level, in that every ecosystem is balanced and all species are in some way dependent on one another to survive, the Buddha meant it on a spiritual level as well, at the level of ultimate reality. We imagine that we are different, that we exist as beings separate from all that surrounds us, but according to the Buddha, it is only a trick of the brain that creates this perception of individuality.

When you perceive a flower, a cat, your brother-in-law Ed, that being you perceive exists at that moment in your mind. Buddhists believe that what exists in your mind is reality, that it is not just a reflection of reality, so if reality exists in your mind, then everything that is part of reality is part of you.

Are you following? This "mind is reality" stuff may be the slipperiest of all Buddhist concepts, and though at times I think I grasp it, my understanding lasts for about one second. And then I lose it again, like when you mean to ask a question, are interrupted, and then walk around all day wondering, "What was it I meant to ask?"

The realization of nonduality, the ultimate understanding of interconnectedness, is what the Buddha experienced one day under his bodhi tree. When you, finally and truly, realize your own connection to all beings, all of everything, then you, too, are enlightened.

IN ANY CASE, in Buddhist terms, I am you, you are me, we are both Mugsy, the big brown dog that limps through my neighborhood, and we are the insects, the cows and chickens, the trees, and they are us. We are all one another, and we are all Buddhas, or at least potential Buddhas. Or as a fellow named Jesus once said, "Lift the stone and you will find me; cleave the wood and I am there."

So it follows that if all sentient beings are potential Buddhas, they are not to be harmed.

Buddhists interpret this in interesting ways.

The writer Natalie Goldberg admits that she used to leave rice on the floor of her Minneapolis apartment for the sentient creatures that lived there, until one day she realized that her compassion was creating a herd of mice. A Buddhist health-care worker in Atlanta traps "all live rodents" in her home, and releases them in the wild. A small sect of Asian monks wear surgical masks day in and day out, so as not to mistakenly inhale some poor sentient creature, and thus bring it to an untimely death.

As a fledgling Buddhist myself, I didn't want to wander through my rosebushes all summer squeezing the leaf-chewing aphids between my fingers, because the aphids are sentient beings, but I didn't want to see the roses suffer either. So I bought a bag of ladybugs. Being Buddhist isn't easy.

ABOUT AN HOUR after I brought Sid inside on my shirtsleeve, it occurred to me that, though he seemed happy enough exploring my CD collection, he was unlikely to find any aphids in my office, and though he had access to more Papermate pens and Post-it Notes than the average ladybug could even dream about, he would probably die of hunger.

So I took him back outside to join the legions of other ladybugs, except I couldn't find them. The cotton bag was empty, the bush near the bag was empty, and I panicked.

Maybe someone had come along and eaten them all in one fell swoop—an anteater maybe, though admittedly there aren't many anteaters in Central Pennsylvania. I hunted through the rosebushes and thick vegetation of my perennial patch, couldn't find a single bug, then turned over the leaves of my veronica and there they were—hundreds of them, hiding in the shade. I introduced Sid to his old friends, and lifted him gently to join them.

When I looked around more closely, I saw that the ladybugs were slowly being warmed back into wakefulness, and were starting to circulate, spreading further out into the garden. Two were copulating on the black raspberry bush. One was doing a kamikaze flight pattern above my pepper seedlings.

This is it, I thought, the perfect compromise. The ladybugs would keep the leaf-chewers in check, and I would accumulate no bad *karma*.

EXCEPT BY THE end of the day, when I went out once more, the ladybugs were gone again. Even the undersides of the leaves were bare of orange-and-black buggies. I looked everywhere, on every bush and tree in my yard, but they had taken to serious hiding—a reasonable response, actually, given what they had been through—snatched in the Sierra foothills, crawl-cleaned, shoved into bags, crated, shipped, refrigerated, then set loose on some weird plants by some odd big fellow who insisted on speaking to them as if they understood.

I searched for ten minutes, saw one ladybug on a leaf, but she turned out to be dead.

So I went inside, reread the release instructions.

"Ladybugs are difficult to see when they are at work," the green flyer warned, which may or may not have been a polite way of saying, "Guess what, doofus—bugs fly."

Guess what else?

The Dalai Lama eats meat.

Nearly all of the various reincarnate lamas eat meat.

Nearly all Tibetans eat meat.

A number of Zen monks eat meat.

The Buddha ate meat. He may, in fact, have died eating a piece of bad pork.

There is a misconception rampant upon the land that all Buddhists are vegetarians. Upon beginning my own exploration of the *dharma,* more than a handful of incredulous friends assumed that my research into Buddhism meant I would be forsaking all of my favorite foods. "What do Buddhists eat?" people kept asking me, as if *this* was the central mystery of the whole religion. "Really, tell me, what do Buddhists eat?"

Westerners have this obsession with food, and we also have a fairly comic-book-level understanding of *karma,* and of the rule not to kill. Due to this, we wrongly assume that Buddhists can't eat anything that might object to being eaten.

If you have a fairly shallow understanding of sentience, you might then assume that Buddhists forswear chicken, pork, beef, and probably fish, too, unless the fish are really, really stupid. If you have a somewhat deeper understanding of sentience, you might include all plant life as well, rice even, because plant life may on some level be sentient—have feelings. I knew a woman once, Trinka, who claimed she could hear a carrot cry when she chopped into it.

So when someone asks me, "What *do* Buddhists eat?" I imagine what they mean is, "What doesn't object to being killed and eaten? Cardboard?"

AH, BUT LIKE so many things in the Buddha way, it is not so simple.

There is always a problem establishing the exact meaning of the Buddha's earliest teachings. They were transmitted orally for some time before anyone wrote them down, and since then they have been passed back and forth from language to language to language. There is no videotape of the Buddha laying down his precepts, and even if there were, the words he spoke 2,500 years ago, in Maghadi or another of the Pali-related dialects of the middle Ganges region, would undoubtedly have very different shadings of meaning from the Pali we understand today.

In following the Buddha's teachings, then, most thoughtful Buddhists I have encountered pretty much accept two givens:

1. Killing is not the only issue. It is best to not even *harm* any sentient being wherever it is avoidable.
2. It is unavoidable. Sentient beings are everywhere, and we are always harming them.

You can't breathe without harming some microscopic being. You can't take a walk out your backdoor without stepping on an insect. As John Daido Loori has pointed out, our body itself is constantly attacking and hopefully destroying viruses. Viruses have life. Maybe they are sentient. Even the staunchest organic vegetarian causes great harm. The very act of tilling the soil plows up innumerable bugs and worms, and the birds tear them apart faster than you can say, "Oops, sorry. Does that count against my *karma*?"

SO WHAT IS a poor Buddhist to do? Sit still, stop breathing? Then you die, and in that way, you harm one very big sentient being. Yourself. We are not to knowingly harm ourselves either.

What is left is what wise Buddhists call the Middle Way. Others call it common sense. You can't end suffering. You can't avoid harming, even killing, small and medium creatures in the course of living a normal life. But don't be thoughtless about it. Avoid stepping on that ant, if you see him there. Open your screen door and whisk the fly out into the yard, instead of swatting first and asking questions later. If it is feasible for you to trap that mouse and set him free out in the woods, consider whether it might be best to do that, but know also that plenty of monasteries have cats.

"It is the cat's *karma* to kill the mouse," one Zen master said. "I am only allowing him to realize his *karma*."

MOREOVER, THE BUDDHIST vow to "save" all sentient beings not only means preserving their lives wherever possible, but also spreading the Buddha's teachings, becoming an enlightened being, as Geshe-la said in Atlanta, in order to help all other sentient beings themselves become enlightened. You need to stay healthy and energetic to do the work of a *bodhisattva*, so starving to death, eating nothing because nothing is exactly begging to be eaten, would still be breaking the Buddha's laws. You would accumulate negative *karma* for your decision not to eat.

MY PURCHASING OF mail-order ladybugs, in other words, was a misunderstanding of what the Buddha wanted me to do. Not killing the aphids on my roses has a certain romantic and idealistic eco-liberal feel to it, but at the same time I am crushing countless beings every time I wander into my organic garden to pick a ripe tomato. Anyway, under my plan, the aphids would still be dying. It would be my actions that brought the ladybug stormtroopers into the yard, and my *karma* would be inextricably linked to the result.

All of this becomes moot, however, because in the weeks and months that follow my ladybug experiment, I see no sign of them anywhere. Sid is gone, and so are all his ladybug sisters and brothers. I look and look. I look under every leaf, behind every plant, deep in the heart of my perennial bushes, in the morning glory thicket, in early dawn and late dusk and at the height of the sun. Within three days of releasing 4,500 refrigerated ladybug somnambulists in my yard, I can't find one.

What I do notice, though, is an influx of birds—indigo buntings, gray catbirds, red-winged blackbirds—avian types that have heretofore been unseen in my bushes. All the regulars are around, too, the sparrows and robins and jays, but in greater numbers.

So perhaps the birds ate my ladybugs, or maybe a good wind blew the bugs three yards down, where my neighbor Jack is right now wondering why he has no aphids on his roses.

AND, BELIEVE ME, the karmic circle of suffering and life doesn't end there. In response to the visiting birds, my wife and I begin to shovel gallon upon gallon of birdseed out our kitchen door onto the lawn, and this does not go unnoticed by a colony of squirrels, two to start, but seven of them by midsummer, all of them fat and full of sunflower kernels. My daughter begins to name them: Nutkin, Twinkleberry, Nutberry.

The sudden herding of squirrels on our side lawn, of course, eventually attracts the attention of one, then two, and ultimately three stray cats. The feline predators begin slinking out of the small wooded area across the road and circling our yard, finally taking to hiding in the flower beds.

My wife feeds the cats, in order to reduce their suffering. The cats begin to chase the squirrels, and eventually catch one or two of them, and the chatter and crying that results leaves little doubt that someone's suffering has not been reduced at all.

One of these days, one of these cats, with his mouth full of squirrel and his small brain filled with adrenaline, is going to rush right across the road into the path of a North American Van Lines truck, and then what?

Whose suffering has been avoided?

• • •

MAYBE IT IS best to just leave nature to itself. But one good result of all this softhearted wheel-spinning on my part is that it draws me outside.

During the spring and early summer, my home meditation began falling into place much easier than during the dreary days that followed my first Zen Mountain experience. I became at least *semi-regular*. When I did manage to sit, I sat longer. My Theravada retreat with Bhante G. was a big help—I found that letting go of the militaristic, regimental "Zen until it hurts" approach made me much more likely to find some level of calm.

But then I hit another wall. Suddenly, sometime in early July, I once more couldn't sit at all. I not only had trouble breathing on my *zafu* every morning, I had trouble breathing in my daily life. Even during tennis, I was holding my breath, which did little good for my backhand. I was a nervous wreck, on and off the cushion. I was failing again.

Except in my yard.

The Buddha found his peace under a bodhi tree, the tree of enlightenment, in ancient India, literally sitting near the base of the trunk for months and months.

I begin to sit under my own bodhi tree, a massive white oak at the far corner of my vegetable patch, and what I experience is not so much a shutting down of my Monkey Mind as an awakening of it. I stop looking for ladybugs, cease obsessing over my own attempt to alter and control nature's balance, and begin to see for the first time how many other odd and wonderful insects are crawling and slithering about. Heretofore, in my simplistic urban mind, a bug was either an ant, a bee, or a moth, but upon beginning the practice of sitting in my garden, on a newspaper surrounded by tomato branches and herb plants and careening zucchini vines, I realize the sheer enormity of it all. Yellow bugs, red bugs, striped bugs, dotted bugs, ridge-backed blue bugs with elongated antennae, slithering bugs, crawling bugs, flitting bugs, flying what's-its, green crickets, brown crickets, black butterflies, amazing prehistoric miniatures with gaping claws and armored torsos. Instead of swatting them away, killing them instinctively merely for the crime of being a bug, I watch them wander through the bug-size jungle and feel as if I am on a safari. Maybe I am weird, but it is fun.

I start seeing other things, too. My bodhi tree, the white oak, is well over one hundred feet tall, and wisteria vines circle the trunk and intersect the branches to the very top. The wisteria is easy to miss, though, unless you stop and look, unless you turn off the mental signal that says "tree" and really endeavor to see what is there. Eventually I spot a squirrel's nest far up near the top branches, home to the well-fed Nutkin, Twinkleberry, and Nutberry, and begin to discern the path they take down the tree, across the middle branches, through the air to my Chinese chestnut, on to the red maple, and then along my neighbor Stella's fence, to my birdfeeder, using their incredible speed and agility to minimize the time they spend on my cat-infested ground.

My "deep looking" has other benefits. I become more mindful in general, more apt to notice when a colleague is troubled, my wife needs to talk, or my daughter is about to spiral off into a tantrum of overstimulation, and more mindful of my own tantrums and mood swings as well. I am more able to react, too—appropriately and, yes, compassionately. There are distinct advantages to being aware of what is going on around you, and distinct disadvantages to seeing only the forest, and never the individual trees.

ONE DAY I pick up John Daido Loori's book *The Eight Gates of Zen* and discover I am not as much a failure as I thought. In the book,

Daido-shi describes ten stages of spiritual development, linked to a series of ox-herding pictures from ancient China. The ox, Daido-shi writes, represents the true self, our authentic nature as human beings.

In the first picture, and the first stage of spiritual development, the student searches for the ox, filled with questions. Like many students, my own search for the ox, my own mind full of doubts and questions, brought me to the monastery door. In the second stage, the student "discovers footprints" of the ox, or in other words, begins to see that Buddhist training may indeed lead the way to finding the true nature of things. "A student at this point experiences some grounding in concentration and single-pointedness of mind," Daido-shi writes. "The internal dialogue slows down enough so that for short periods of time, during intense stretches of sitting . . . one has the experience of 'body and mind falling away.'" Well, if 'short periods of time' truly qualify, then I have reached this stage. At ZMM and at the Bhavana Society, and in my own yard, I have begun, albeit briefly, to feel that falling away.

In stage three, the ox is sighted, and though the student still may be confused, and is often unsure of exactly what he has seen, "for a very short time, the self is forgotten." In the fourth stage the ox is caught, "seized with great struggle," and, according to Daido-shi, "the student begins to get a rudimentary grasp of the nature of the self, (though) it is still difficult to manifest it in one's life. You know what you should be doing, you know what is right, but that is not what you do."

The fifth stage is taming the ox, and eventually, in the succeeding stages, the student rides the ox home, transcends the ox, transcends the self as well, becomes enlightened, and in the tenth stage, "returns to the world," to become a teacher, to help other sentient beings along their own path to enlightenment.

As ragtag and convoluted as my personal path to Buddhist practice has been, I am by my own skeptical judgment probably straddling the third and fourth stages, and heck, given the overwrought, jittery, hyperactive nature of my Monkey Mind and my own destructive tendency to do six things at once while watching the news, straddling the third and fourth stages seems pretty good.

WHAT DO BUDDHISTS eat?

They eat chicken, pork, beef, rice, noodles, fish, fruit, fudge-striped cookies, Ben and Jerry's Cherry Garcia, just about everything other people eat, though they strive to be more mindful, and to stop when their bellies are full.

How do they justify the death of a sentient cow or chicken?

Much like some Native American tribes revered and hunted the buffalo, Buddhists honor the fish or fowl or mammal that has fallen to fill their plate, and see the eating of food, any food really, even a grape, to be a sort of sacrament.

Buddhists eat well. They—we—have to. It takes considerable energy to achieve final enlightenment, and once we do, there is still the hard work of helping the rest of the sentient world over the numerous hurdles.

PART 3

REAL BUDDHISTS DON'T
TAKE NOTES

11

DESTROY YOUR NEIGHBOR,
DESTROY YOURSELF

The Dalai Lama and the Action Hero

THE HISTORICAL BUDDHA was born a prince, and upon his birth, wise men of old India predicted he would become either a celebrated king or a great spiritual master. The young Buddha's father, King Suddhodana, preferred to keep his only son in the family business, and so constructed palaces filled with food, dancing women, and lovely gardens, hoping that his son might never gain any knowledge of earthly suffering and thus never seek spiritual answers.

Despite the old man's earnest attempts, however, Prince Siddhartha managed during a few spontaneous afternoon forays to witness the *dukkha* in all of us. Bothered by this delayed revelation, the Buddha-to-be left his father's palace once and for all under cover of night, not bothering to wake his wife, Yasodhara, and infant son, Rahula, and disappeared for many, many years.

In late July, I leave, too, under cover of early morning darkness, without waking my wife and daughter, though in contrast to Siddhartha, I *do* tell them where I am going. Renita knows the phone number of my hotel. Poor Yasodhara didn't even get a good-bye note.

Prince Siddhartha headed southeast, toward the river Anoma. I head west, toward the river Mississippi. Though the ladybugs in my garden were a pleasant distraction, I remind myself to stay focused on my initial impulse—my American Buddhism Project—the notion that if I can find how others are fitting this ancient philosophy into their modern American lives, I might better understand the best way to fit it into my own.

I learn from one of my many Buddhist magazines that the Dalai Lama will be visiting Bloomington, Indiana, in late July, and take that as a sign. If John Daido Loori is a living Buddha, then the Dalai Lama is undoubtedly *the* living Buddha, the head man. And if the Hoosiers aren't American, then who is? If Buddhism can thrive out in the rural heartland, I tell myself, then surely it can thrive anywhere. Even inside of me.

On the ride out, of course, I pass vastly more fundamentalist Christian churches than I do Buddhist monasteries. Billboards along every road remind me that JESUS SAVES and JESUS IS COMING SOON, and those little marquees outside of Christian churches quote so much Gospel that I feel I have read the entire New Testament by the time I reach Wheeling.

But there is Buddhism out here, too. *Tricycle's* Dharma Center Directory shows *zendos* and retreat centers in nearly every state of the Union, in the big towns and cities, of course, but also in places like Shelburne, Vermont; Summertown, Tennessee; Yellow Springs, Ohio; and Floyds Knobs, Indiana. And even this extensive listing only shows the formal centers—countless small, informal sitting groups meet in people's homes, and thousands of other people sit alone.

• • •

I DRIVE ALL morning, fervent and focused, finally stopping for coffee at a Waffle House near Plain City, Ohio. My car sports a FREE TIBET bumpersticker that I picked up in Atlanta, and as I lean against the left fender, sipping my cup of mindfulness, a young man spills out of a purple school bus and starts running toward me. He is a 1990s version of a hippie—a white kid with dreadlocks; a knit cap, probably hemp; and Grateful Dead patches on his Levi cutoffs.

"Hey, hey, free Tibet," he shouts, pointing to my bumper. "Free Tibet, man."

"Hey," I answer back.

"Free Tibet," he repeats. "Were you there?"

"Tibet?" I ask.

"No, man. The concert. Were you there?"

I realize he is talking about the Tibetan Freedom Concert held just one month ago in San Francisco, and that to him, the grave situation in Tibet has mainly translated into an opportunity to hear the Red Hot Chili Peppers through really big speakers. I explain that I'm not primarily a music fan, but rather am heading to Bloomington to see His Holiness the Dalai Lama.

The hippie kid tells me that he and his busload of pals are on their way to Woodstock, New York, for another music festival. "It's gonna be cool."

His girlfriend, a twenty-something long-haired young woman in an oversized Mama Cass cotton dress and Birkenstocks, is on a pay phone about twenty feet off from us. She seems to be arguing with someone.

My new friend shouts to her:

"The Dalai Lama is in Bloomington. Wanna go?"

She waves and shouts back. "Free Tibet. I was there."

I give them a peace sign. There is nothing else to be done.

• • •

I AM NOT going to a rock concert, I am headed to a spiritual teaching, though you wouldn't know it from what happens next. As I drive toward western Ohio on Interstate 70, a brown Plymouth Voyager starts honking and pulls up alongside my little car. Six men inside the minivan are waving and gesticulating, and I imagine for a horrible moment that something has fallen from my engine, or perhaps my tailpipe is on fire.

I roll down my window, the front passenger rolls down his, and at seventy miles per hour, he shouts, "ARE . . . YOU . . . GOING . . . TO . . . SEE . . . THE . . . DALAI . . . LAMA."

It was my bumpersticker again. It might as well read BUDDHIST ON BOARD.

"Yes," I shout back, and the passengers bow toward me, a small *gassho*. I don't bow back but grip the wheel, thinking about impermanence, what might happen if the driver decides to *gassho* as well and his Plymouth veers into my Ford. Seven sentient beings rapidly reincarnated.

The Voyager, though, speeds off, and I notice that, for reasons that elude me even now, someone with some aerosol cheese-in-a-can has sprayed the words CHEESE MOBILE onto the minivan's back window. Three men in the rear seat wave through the cheese.

SOME MOMENTS CANNOT be surpassed, and perhaps that is one of them. The drive grows less eventful, and I am left to amuse myself. I ponder how driving down a modern interstate highway is actually a pretty fit metaphor for the manner in which many of us lead our lives—we are rushing, always thinking of the future, of our destination, focusing on what is four hours, or four hundred miles, or four years ahead, and constantly missing what is right there, just then, at the moment.

Even if we see the passing trees, the buildings, the sky, we don't *really* see them—we are going way too fast to do anything more than register them as abstract concepts. Tree. Building. Corn. The only sentient beings that come into our awareness are those that *squoosh* into our windshield, or go *plop-squish-plop* under our wheels.

Modern highways, in fact, all fenced and landscaped and isolated, are intentionally designed to help us miss things, to assist us in avoiding trees, farmhouses, uneven terrain, just as our modern lives are increasingly arranged, often scheduled down to the nanosecond, to help us avoid surprise, discomfort, boredom, contemplation.

Approaching Indiana, a state that bills itself as the Crossroads of America, I make the decision to bail out of the interstate system, dip down through Dayton, and pick up old Highway 44, a two-lane scenic meander through infinite fields of mid-summer corn, contented cows, and some of the largest, most beautiful farmhouses I have ever seen.

I attempt to be mindful and really notice what I am passing, not just the asphalt stretched out before my nose. My goal is not so hard to accomplish—you can smell the farm soil here, the sky is crystal blue with cheerful white clouds, and every third house, it seems, has a happy family seated on the lawn, holding a yard sale. I honk and wave at each one I pass.

Slowing down through small town after small town, I am not "making time," but I am better enjoying the time I do spend getting to my destination. In Connersville, Indiana, I go by Scripture Chevrolet, where a sign reads, IT'S OK TO WANT A REALLY COOL CAR. Well, I think, that's grasping, and grasping leads to discontent, and discontent leads to all suffering, so I figure the Scripture Chevy dealer isn't a Buddhist.

Then, a few miles further up the road, I pass a Methodist Church. A small sign on the front lawn proclaims THE MOST BEAUTIFUL PEOPLE REFLECT CHRIST.

Well, probably no Buddhists in there either, but it is a sentiment many Buddhists would find agreeable. As Thich Nhat Hanh often reminds us, we are all Buddhas-to-be.

IN MARTINSVILLE, I stop for dinner at the Happy Buddha Chinese Restaurant, just off the square. A television set dominates the one-room dining area, so we needn't be bored, or too mindful of our food. The local news is on, Eyewitness 13 from Indianapolis, and while I'm waiting for my sweet and sour soup, the Dalai Lama appears on the screen, bowing and smiling.

A reporter's voice-over talks about His Holiness's upcoming visit to the Indiana University campus, and then a female anchor looks earnestly toward the camera. "Be sure to tune in tomorrow," she reminds us, "when I will have an exclusive one-on-one with the Dalai Lama."

The Chinese-American waitress, a girl of probably only fifteen, has stopped and is watching the television with me.

"Do you know the Dalai Lama?" I ask her.

"Who?" she answers, seemingly embarrassed by my direct, perhaps impertinent question.

"The Dalai Lama."

"Is he Chinese?" she ventures.

"No, he is Tibetan."

"Oh!" She shakes her head. "No, I do not know him."

I attempt to explain that I am talking about the fellow on the television, and that I never thought she knew him personally but merely wondered if she was aware of his teachings and his visit to the nearby Bloomington campus, but she flushes and runs back to the kitchen.

For the entire rest of the meal, her suspicious mother waits on me.

THE FOLLOWING MORNING, I see His Holiness.

He arrives on the Indiana University campus in a police motorcade, sirens blaring and red lights flashing, flanked by impressive motorcycles, just like in the movies. Out of the various nondescript black sedans pours a squadron of plainclothes police officers, looking just like Secret Service, but actually members of the Bloomington Critical Incident Response Team. (The Dalai Lama, exiled king of Tibet, does not get actual Secret Service protection, because the U.S. State Department does not recognize him as a legitimate foreign ruler. It all has to do with not angering China and upsetting the trade imbalance.)

Once the blue-suited, sunglassed CIRT cops determine that the area is secure and trade this information with one another through countless walkie-talkies, a few young monks come out of the cars, followed by the action movie star Steven Seagal, and then the Dalai Lama himself, bowing and smiling. The security seems a bit overdone for a simple Buddhist monk, but the Dalai Lama has his enemies.

Dressed in traditional red-and-yellow robes and less traditional rubber-soled Rockport oxfords, the Dalai Lama undertakes his first official chore of the day—planting a spruce tree. Actually, he just turns a small shovel of dirt on a hillside, near where Indiana University landscapers will eventually come in and do the actual planting with big machines, but that is how tree-planting ceremonies go these days.

Then fifty or so high school students, participants in a youth peace and ecology conference, take turns reading bits and pieces of a poem while the Dalai Lama beams in their direction. I am about five feet away from the reincarnate master, and to be honest, I am mesmerized. Even the most jaded and cynical observer would have to admit that this fellow radiates pleasant vibrations.

Following the poem, the Dalai Lama blesses individual scarves for each of the high school ecology activists, and smiles that much more when they return the favor by offering their awkward attempts at the *gassho* bow. The kids are amusing, and he seems to be amused.

Then he addresses the group, opening with the observation that despite all the bad news in the world, the destruction of so many of our natural resources, the sight of actively engaged young people gives him hope.

"This small planet is our only home," he tells them in his uncertain English. "Although we have technology to reach moon and possibly some other stars, I think that at least for several generations there is no hope to settle there. Whole humanity live on new planet is for time being impossible, so this is our *only* home. So while we are always making some complaint—for instance here today, I've been complaining too hot, too humidity—this is our only home, so we have to take care."

The young people laugh and smile at the humidity joke. It is late July, and even the bugs are sweating.

"Now my generation," the sixty-one-year-old leader continues, "we are almost begin to say good-bye to this world. Year by year, we are getting older and older, so whether we enjoy it or not, as Buddhists, we are looking forward to another life. So then the younger generation, now you have to face the consequences of a long future, so that lays the responsibility naturally on your shoulder."

The high school students seem pleased, then stunned, and eventually frightened. The Dalai Lama has essentially said to them, "We give up. You fix it."

FOLLOWING THE TREE planting, the kids go off with their scarves and "the media" is herded toward the IU Memorial Union. I have finagled my way into a press pass, and follow along, anxious to get a closer look at His Holiness. Before I can enter the large conference room, however, police dogs sniff my briefcase for bombs. The security measures are being taken seriously.

I find myself sitting next to the Eyewitness 13 anchorwoman who just the evening before promised her viewers an exclusive "one-on-one." She seems bored and pages through her press packet with a vague air of disgust about her. Most of the media are from the state's larger newspapers and television outlets, but a few are long-haired, beaded reporters from various Buddhist alternative magazines, the very ones I subscribed to when I first embarked on this Project. Maybe the blond anchorwoman resents the fact that the Buddhist media members have hogged all the front seats.

The first question posed to His Holiness, not surprisingly, has to do with China, and the various calls for an economic boycott related to Tibetan human rights.

The Dalai Lama, though, surprises me with his answer.

"Basically, China should not isolate," he says. "China is a most important nation already and no doubt next century will be a very important member of the human community, so China must be brought into the mainstream. Another thing, some people want to containment China—" away from the microphone, His Holiness engages in a brief discussion with his secretary, who also serves as an occasional interpreter, and then continues "—they want to contain China. That is not only practically difficult, but morally wrong. It is a big nation, more than one point two billions of human beings, so they have every right to more prosperity. So now, therefore, I think the effective method is making good friends, good relations, meantime in certain principle matters, remaining very firm, very clear." He smiles and bows. "Of course, I am not expert."

Though many exiled Tibetans disagree with his stance, the Dalai Lama has become increasingly conciliatory over his many years of exile. He makes it clear that he sees Tibet as a separate nation according to international law, now an "occupied land," but rather than insist on complete Chinese withdrawal, the Buddhist leader and walking symbol of compassion and nonattachment explains to the press that he is open to "a Middle Way approach; not complete separation, but something mutually agreeable." Perhaps, he has suggested elsewhere, Tibet could be an autonomous Chinese Republic.

His Holiness takes a sip of water, then looks out toward the sea of cameras and waving hands and points directly at me.

I am caught off guard, and entirely delighted. Here he is, the Buddha of living Buddhas, and here I am, Mister Monkey Mind, the doofus of *dokusan,* an errant altar boy, with a chance to ask the man anything I want. I embarked on this Project intent on answering a fairly basic question, and now I have the opportunity to simply ask that question of the source. It feels like a climactic moment.

"What place," I inquire of his Holiness, "do you see for Buddhism in modern America? Where does it fit?"

He stops to think before answering, then smiles at me warmly. "Basically," he says, "I consider America to be a Judeo-Christian country, so my feeling, it is better to keep your traditional values, including your traditional Judeo-Christian religion."

I smile and nod. He smiles back, and then I realize he has said no, it doesn't fit at all, and we don't belong. The air goes dashing out of my balloon, and I suspect, out of the collective balloons of all the earnest Buddhists clogging the front rows of seats. He doesn't want us? We have to go back to church?

"But some people," His Holiness continues after a moment's thought, "maybe the Buddhist approach, they find more acceptable. In such case, if you think this new approach is more effective, then it is your right to adopt this new system as your own religion. Then another thing, you see, in order to justify your decision, there is sometimes the tendency to criticize your previous view. That, I think you must avoid." He nods sharply. I feel pangs of guilt.

"Then of course, study is very important," he goes on. "I often get the impression sometimes that small things"—he points to the *mala* on his wrist, the wooden, rosarylike bracelet that many American Buddhists wear—"becomes your main practice, but the basic Buddhist teaching, and the understanding of meditation, gets neglected. No. You must have knowledge, understanding of basic Buddhist teachings."

We have been given a reprieve.

The Olympics are underway in Atlanta, and some reporter in the front row can't resist asking His Holiness if he thinks Tibet will ever have an Olympic delegation.

"I don't know," he says, and smiles broadly. People begin to laugh, but the Dalai Lama is not finished answering. He pushes out his chest a bit and suggests that Tibetans might do well in running events. "Some people who are born in higher altitudes, their lungs are better equipped."

The Channel 13 anchorwoman is truly disgusted now. The Dalai Lama's views on track and field, perhaps, do not strike her as newsworthy. She lets out a bit of a snort after the next question.

"Do you think," one of the Buddhist media asks, "that human consciousness is evolving?"

The Dalai Lama's secretary interprets the question for him, and then His Holiness answers in English. "Yes," he says, leaning forward with enthusiasm. "The concept of 'our interest and their interest' is on the wane. The modern world is becoming smaller and smaller, and especially in modern economy, natural boundaries mean nothing. So that's now reality. We have to treat whole world as one world or one human community, so therefore upon that basis in reality there is no possibility of 'our interest, their interest' or 'our victory, their defeat.' Today, in modern world, to destroy your neighbor or enemy means to destroy yourself. If your neighbor suffers, great destructions happen, eventually it is your burden, it will ruin your economy. So therefore, the only proper method to solve problems is dialogue, compromise. The nonviolent method is the only way to solve human conflict. I think we need to make no room to use violence."

I glance over at Steven Seagal, the avenging action movie hero, star of *Marked for Death, Hard to Kill,* and *The Glimmer Man.* Seagal, as he listens to the Dalai Lama's admonitions, looks a bit dyspeptic. He has been at His Holiness's side, more or less, for most of the day, but no one has really acknowledged him, he hasn't spoken, and given the heavy police presence, his martial arts skills are unlikely to come into play. He winces a lot, purses his lips, and generally has the look of someone who is not sure why he is there.

THE DALAI LAMA is Tibet's exiled spiritual leader and, prior to his exile, was also the country's secular leader. He is occasionally referred to by the Western media as Tibet's God-King, though the "God" part is not at all accurate.

He is a reincarnate lama, the fourteenth *Dalai* Lama, and Dalai Lamas rank above all the others, but rather than a god, he is a *bodhisattva,* the Buddhist term for one who is on the path to enlightenment, or Buddhahood, a journey that Tibetan Buddhists believe can span millions of lifetimes.

The Dalai Lama is highly revered, believed to be much further up the reincarnation ladder than the rest of us, but he is mortal. Born in Tibet in 1935 to peasant parents, he was recognized at the age of two as the reincarnation of the previous Dalai Lama and assumed full political power at age fifteen, with China already growling at the door.

How young boys are recognized as reincarnations of old Buddhist men is particularly intriguing to outsiders; it is an enigmatic process, involving mystical signs, visions in lake water, the casting about of balls of barley dough, and much chanting. Moreover, it is said that the young boys who are identified as these reincarnated souls often remember their past lives, or recognize people or objects connected to their previous incarnations. Tibetans take reincarnation very seriously.

By the age of nineteen, around the age that I started dating, the fourteenth Dalai Lama was negotiating his country's future with the likes of Mao Tse-tung, Deng Xiaoping, and other Chinese leaders. In 1959, when the Chinese occupation of Tibet led to a national uprising, the Dalai Lama feared for his own life and fled his home country, at night, in disguise, into Northern India. He and his government-in-exile have resided in Dharamsala, India, ever since, yet despite years of effort, endless travel, and a Nobel peace prize, he has so far been unable to convince the outside world to devote much more than lip service to Tibetan independence.

KEEPING THE CAUSE of Tibet alive in our minds is one of the reasons His Holiness is visiting Indiana. Two others are to help lay the cornerstone for the Tsong Kha Sanctuary, an international Buddhist temple for peace and compassion to be based in Bloomington, and to visit his brother.

Thubten J. Norbu, elder brother to the Dalai Lama and a lesser reincarnate lama in his own right, is a retired Indiana University professor of Uralic studies. He was thirteen when monks came to his family home in northeast Tibet and started testing his two-year-old baby brother to see if little Tenzin was perhaps their new leader. Norbu fled Tibet about thirty years ago, when the Chinese asked him to help assassinate his brother.

To help finance his brother's current visit, Norbu has arranged for the university to sponsor a free public appearance, and the line for this event begins forming four hours early. By the time I arrive, it snakes around the massive auditorium, out into the street, and right down the road, past a complex of gymnasium buildings.

The auditorium holds 3,700 people, but these seats fill quickly, so university officials open three separate overflow rooms, where a few thousand more people watch His Holiness on a video hookup.

Before coming to Bloomington, I had spoken to a friend of mine in California, a reporter for a Bay Area newspaper. "You are going to see His Holiness?" he said. "That guy is like Mick Jagger out here."

Now I know what he means. The large crowd has traveled in from all over, and they buzz with preconcert excitement, clutching *malas,* waving to their friends in the balcony, proudly displaying their BOY-COTT CHINA T-shirts. The assembly is fairly diverse—white, black, and Asian, a contingent of college kids, a fair number of baby boomers, some Tibetan monks, some Zen monks, a few Christian clergy.

As His Holiness is introduced by a university official, he, too, waves to some old friends in the front row, a contingent of aging fellows in orange robes. Then he takes the microphone, and says, "You see, I speak in broken English, which gets more broken as I get older, so you should not expect much."

The audience roars with laughter. The exiled Tibetan leader has good comic timing, and laughing eyes, and he likes to tease.

His theme for the evening, he tells us, is "Overcoming Differences." He speaks first about religion.

"Among humanity, there are many different religious traditions, so you see, no single religion could satisfy everyone." He likens the variety of religions to a restaurant menu—if a restaurant were to serve just one dish for breakfast, lunch, and dinner, he says, the number of customers would "fast reduce."

"So we have restaurants that serve American food, and French food, and Chinese food, and Indian food, and Tibetan." He pauses, smiles broadly to signal a joke. "Well, maybe not so much Tibetan."

The audience laughs. The Dalai Lama's sister-in-law, a friendly smiling woman that people in town call Mrs. Norbu, runs a Tibetan restaurant in Bloomington. I hope His Holiness has not offended her by suggesting that Tibetan cooking is not so popular in these parts. Sisters-in-law can be touchy about such comments, even coming from a reincarnate master.

"You see," he explains, finishing his metaphor, "religion is the food of consciousness, and just like we have many foods, it's good to have so many religions."

Moving on to the subject of nationality differences, the Dalai Lama echoes some of his thoughts from the earlier press conference. "The world is now much smaller," he says. "We are all much more dependent on one another." He cites ecological issues such as global warming and acid rain that pay no attention to national borders, and he mentions the growth of international trade. "Now your neighbor's development is very much connected to your development, and your neighbor's economy is very much dependent on your economy. Once you realize this, it is very simple to overcome difficulties with your neighbors."

His politics of mutually agreeable reconciliation, I realize, is just another form of nondualistic thinking. If you swat that fly, you are swatting yourself. If you destroy your neighbor's economy, you are flooded with refugees, and your own economy suffers. Drop an atom bomb, and the nuclear fallout drifts globally. *Karma* happens.

"The concept of war," he says, "the concept of using force, I think now has become old-fashioned."

He draws protracted applause, and then calls on everyone listening to develop compassion. "As compassion develops, you gradually reduce hate. I call this inner disarmament. More compassion means less anger, and less anger means less fear," he tells us. "And less fear equals a happy life!"

I am buying it, but I notice the fellow directly to my left has fallen asleep. I consider whether nudging him would be more or less compassionate. I opt for not worrying about it, and let the guy snooze.

"When I was young," the Dalai Lama tells us, "I was very short-tempered, but at the age of sixteen, I started to take a serious interest in the study of *dharma*. I can say through my own experience, yes, we can change the mind. You can become a much more calm person, much happier.

"But always in America someone will ask me, 'What is the best way, what is the quickest?'" He pauses, smiles again, looks directly at his American audience. "But you see, there is no quick way. It takes effort."

He wraps up quickly after that, checking his watch a few times, then saying, "So that is about my time. If you think some of my points are interesting, please study and analyze them. If you think these points are nonsense, then just forget it."

SATURDAY MORNING, IT is clear that at least a few in the audience found His Holiness to be interesting. Tickets to see the Dalai Lama lay the cornerstone for the new Tsong Kha Sanctuary and to hear him perform *Sem-Ke*, the ritual for Aspirational *Bodhicitta*, are $40 for a back seat and $100 for the front, and even at those prices, roughly a thousand people show up, early, in thick fog.

We are herded across a massive lawn, past the Tibetan Cultural Center, to a large white tent facing an ornate altar. Security is tighter than ever, and a certain air of gravity hangs over us. Just hours before, a bomb exploded in Atlanta's Centennial Olympic Park, killing two people.

I count fourteen CIRT officers in blue suits ringing the stage area, staring off into the woods, talking into little microphones, and at least six additional brown-uniformed Monroe County sheriff's deputies. And of course, there are more police behind us, and even more out on Snoddy Road, directing traffic.

The Dalai Lama takes his place on the altar, and is joined by a few monks for a long spell of Tibetan chanting. The voices are low-pitched and lovely, an enchanting oral rumble. Then he begins the *Sem-Ke,* which, it turns out, is basically another sermon, a long, complicated scriptural interpretation delineating some of the finer points of enlightenment and compassion.

Like Geshe Lobsang Tenzin Negi at the La Hacienda retreat, the Dalai Lama speaks to his audience more than he meditates with them. Unlike Geshe-la, however, His Holiness, I notice, begins most events about five to ten minutes early.

Sitting high on the altar, the Dalai Lama speaks Tibetan this morning, and his words come to us through an interpreter. We are continually recycled, reincarnated, he tells us, and the only way out of this constant cycle is to gain full enlightenment. Even if we do gain full enlightenment, however, we might not end our cycle of reincarnation, because we may very well choose to stick around, in order to help others gain enlightenment.

I listen and begin to wonder if he is perhaps talking about himself. He certainly seems more enlightened than anyone I know, but I'm not sure if he counts himself among the fully enlightened or not. Maybe *that* is what I should have asked him.

The next ten minutes or so, His Holiness delves into a discussion of "the nature of reality," the continually perplexing questions of whether things exist separate from the self, how we know of their existence, and what is and is not real? His Holiness is into some pretty deep intellectual territory for a Saturday morning, and though the audience is politely attentive, I imagine more than a few of us would have welcomed a bit more incense, ritual, chanting, and some Tibetan horns.

The Dalai Lama is once again stressing to his American audience that "this Buddhism" is actually a lot of hard work. Not only do you have to sit and wrestle with the agile and energetic brain monkey, but you have to strive toward an understanding of deep philosophical teachings, such as the "misconception of inherent existence."

That misconception, he explains, is our tendency toward dualism, our belief that the phenomena we experience externally exist in their own right, that they are separate from us. "Inside our minds we have a strong sense that these internal and external phenomenon do indeed exist the way they appear," His Holiness says. "But this is wrong."

He shakes his head side to side. "What we are doing is misconceiving the nature of ourselves and others, self and other appearing to inherently exist, whereas they don't, but we go right along with that appearance . . . and in dependence on that, generate afflictive emotions that themselves induce contaminated *karmas*."

Whew! It does get deep.

Let me attempt to translate the translation.

I think what the Dalai Lama is talking about is our belief that we are different than everything else, that there is a "me," and that that "me" is an independent entity distinct from our girlfriend, or our dog, or the fellow up the road with the big house and the shiny new car. When our girlfriend displeases us somehow, by snapping her gum, or not caring enough, or going away, we imagine that "she" has acted independently, and wish "she" would change her actions. So we get angry, unhappy, mean—the afflictive emotions. But in a Buddhist's mind, "she" is just "us," and "we" are just "her"—you and she basically exist in the same place, your mind—and to be angry at her makes no more sense than to be angry at your head for going bald. It is just what happens, it is how your body works. Likewise, there is no use wishing you had a nice house and shiny new car like the fellow up the road. "You" are "he," and "he" is "you," and you already have it.

In a manner of speaking, of course. This is not to say you can walk in, take the guy's keys, and drive off. What the Dalai Lama is promoting here is a way of looking at things, a manner of viewing the world around us that not only promotes compassion, and helpful action, but decreases negativity and angst.

Why be miserable? Where's the future in it?

You can shout at the rush hour traffic, bang the dashboard, twist your bowel into a knot, or you can say, "That is just the traffic, and it is the way the traffic is."

But, you say, the traffic makes you late.

How can you be late? You are right where you should be.

AND IF YOU are right where you should be, why are you chasing the Dalai Lama around Bloomington with a pen and a pad of paper? It dawns on me as His Holiness continues outlining the basic Tibetan Buddhist philosophy that my initial idea for this Project was altogether Monkey-Minded. Dualistic. Very Western. Fairly anal. Instead of "just sitting" as John Daido Loori first instructed, I have wasted months attempting to track down the right weekend seminar, the "correct" answer, some sort of instant *karma*. If there is no difference between "me" and all these other Buddhists, why am I hurrying about trying to meet them?

I am beginning to feel very *unenlightened*—further away from any understanding, further away from any clear answer than when I started my Project Mind. What was the question, anyway? This is Buddhism in America, plainly, but it is Tibetan Buddhism in America. Ninety percent of the audience is white, Western, and probably raised Christian or Jew, and 90 percent of us don't really seem to fit in. We are spectators, crowded around the select few monks. *Dharma* theater.

My Monkey Mind goes into chastisement mode again, and what it says to me this time is, *You shallow ignoramus! Thought all you had to do was get within three feet of His Holiness and you'd find enlightenment through osmosis? What did you expect, a contact high? This is a twenty-five-hundred-year-old religion, and you hope to conquer it with a twenty-five-minute attention span? Real Buddhists don't take notes.*

Lucky for me, I'm distracted from these thoughts when three or four large yellow butterflies flutter through the field, landing on the plainclothes police officers right behind His Holiness. I forget my inner turmoil, ignore the unkind Monkey, and watch Steven Seagal again. The action movie hero has still not spoken a word, though he is billed as the "host" of the morning event. He looks pretty sour-faced and uncomfortable, and seems to wander out of his way to avoid the press corps. The Dalai Lama keeps warning against violence, and I keep looking at Seagal, whose "Buddhist" film characters slice throats with credit cards. I am wondering what Seagal can be thinking. I know why he is here—the Dalai Lama is smart enough to know that movie stars such as Seagal and Richard Gere draw television cameras and slick magazine writers, and this leads to further exposure for the Tibetan cause, which might get China to concede something sooner or later. Does Seagal know why he is here? Has it just dawned on him?

Maybe I am just projecting. I'm not even sure why *I'm* here anymore. And surely I am violating one of the basic Buddhist precepts—Right Speech, do not speak of other's faults. For all I know, Seagal may be an excellent Buddhist off-screen, and God knows I'm far from perfect.

UP ON THE altar, the Dalai Lama is checking his watch again. "So now, that's about it for today's teaching," he says, switching back to English.

As part of the Bodhicitta, we all join him in reciting a prayer, "The Key to Purifying Misdeeds and Accumulating Merit," and he finishes with a final admonition.

"Some will say, 'Oh, I want to achieve Buddhahood in order to benefit others,' but then they desire to achieve Buddhahood within three years, or say six years, or nine years," His Holiness tells us, smiling gently, seeming, like many of my other Buddhist teachers, to have somehow read my thoughts. "I think that's nonsense. That sort of attitude is really dangerous. But count in eons, eons, that's really helpful, that helps us to gain determination. So count eons, rather than hours or weeks or months."

Eons?

Thousands upon thousands of years?

Heck.

Maybe I'm not that far behind after all.

12

TRYING TO HIT THE BALL

....

Fruitless Searching on the Fruited Plain

LEAVING BLOOMINGTON, I avoid the major highways again, instead driving north past flat farms, weathered houses, grain silos, and small Indiana towns like Carp, Brick Chapel, and Belshaw. Radio stations are few and far between here, but I manage to pull in a signal from Chicago, and eavesdrop on the final three innings of a White Sox game.

The Sox enter the eighth with a one-run lead and seem on the verge of turning around what the announcer tells us has been a disastrous homestand, but the Texas Rangers stubbornly tie it up before the inning ends. Not much happens in the ninth, so the game goes into overtime.

In the tenth inning, Sox reliever Bill Simas walks Ranger pinch-hitter Kurt Stillwell, and I think *karma*. Simas has taken an action—throwing four times outside the strike zone, and not cleverly enough to fool the batter—and anyone who knows the game of baseball knows that this action is bound to result in some future pain or suffering.

Sure enough, Ranger first baseman Lee Stevens is up next and triples into the left corner, sending Stillwell home for what turns out to be the game-winning run. The pitcher's negative action has an instant undesirable consequence for Chicago fans.

I don't know if Geshe Michael Roach, the American-born Tibetan monk who entertained at Change Your Mind Day, is a baseball fan, but for the moment I wish he and I were both at the game, grinning in the warm sun, cracking open peanuts, and shouting, *"Dooooooooooh-chett!"*

BASEBALL CAN BE very Buddhist.

Eugene Herrigel, in his classic *Zen in the Art of Archery,* stresses the ultimate goal of "letting the shot loose itself," the importance of not taking aim. Many baseball players have expressed similar theories of hitting—try too hard, and the desired result eludes you. Yogi Berra, an unintentional Zen Roshi, is said to have asked, "How can you think and hit at the same time?"

Indeed. How can you? This is the essence of the practice. Sit yourself on the cushion, day in and day out, but don't grip, don't attach, don't strive for enlightenment, or it will never come. Sox pitcher Bill Simas probably aimed too hard, and that's why Lee Stevens could triple.

Well, I am aiming way too hard—that much has become clear. Ignoring Roshi Yogi's wise advice, I am trying to think and hit at the same time, and my whole Project is probably a waste of effort. I could observe two million, six million, eight million American Buddhists, and be no closer to any real understanding.

• • •

TO DISTRACT MYSELF from this grim realization, I stop in Chicago and get a ticket to the next day's ballgame. Sunday afternoon, the Sox engage in one last session of *dharma* combat with the Texas Rangers.

I want to be distracted, and the new Comiskey is just the place. Fans mill about, as if incontinent. The beer man shouts, "Beah heah, beah heah." The hot dog man hollers, "hoot doogs." The soda man hollers something I can't quite make out, and the kid in the seat next to me tries to encase his entire head in cotton candy. Somewhere on the field, there is a game going on.

I have good seats, but my view is blocked almost constantly, so in a rare Buddhist moment I leave the lower deck and climb up to the empty expanse of the nosebleed section, where I can actually see something. The game goes on, pitch by pitch, small karmic event after small karmic event, and since I am unable to make out at such a distance who is actually at bat, or who is advancing to what base, I focus more on the angles and rhythms of the game.

It occurs to me, watching the little figures scurrying around on the field, that professional athletes are the sacred monks of American society. We lack discipline ourselves, but count on them to have it. They enact their complex rituals in our name. And as a result, if they perform well, we honor them. We honor them pretty well, in fact. Their begging bowls are full.

Eventually I snap out of my reverie and see that it is the eighth inning already. Though it is mid-day, the stadium lights have been switched on to counter thick gray rain clouds arriving from the west.

The Sox are up 3–1.

Slowly but surely, the clouds roll in, the lightning comes, the downpour arrives in sheets, and the umpires call the game.

Karma.

There was nothing any of us could do to stop it.

ANOTHER OMEN? THE washed-out inning seems like one, only this time the omen is against me. I drive nearly an hour through the pouring rain to Downers Grove, an affluent western suburb, until the sky clears, and the humidity becomes unbearable. I have scheduled a meeting with yet another group of Buddhists, and though I've all but abandoned any interest in my Project, I am mindful enough of what the nuns taught me about manners to not skip my appointments.

On Lyman Street, I find a well-maintained ranch home owned by Tom and Sue Wolsko, and pull into the driveway. Someone has done a lot of work on the flower gardens.

Tom and Sue are part of a meditation group that doesn't even have a name, it is so small. The group meets once a week, on Sunday evenings, in someone's home, usually Tom and Sue's home. Jack Hatfield's car rolls into the driveway just behind me, and there is an awkward moment as we realize that Tom and Sue are just sitting down to a late dinner. No one gets too upset though, and we work it out easily—Tom and Sue eat, Jack joins them for a snack, and I, glutted with Comiskey's popcorn and hot dogs, sit at the kitchen table with a glass of water.

Then we adjourn to the family room, which looks just like any other comfortable suburban family room, except for a few *zafus* on the polished wood floor. As we meditate together, I hear the voices of the neighborhood kids playing some game. One of the kids is banging on a garbage can, another is bouncing a basketball. Despite the distractions, it feels good to sit meditation again, even in this very unmonastic setting. I don't come up with any answers to anything, but it is a very soothing twenty-five minutes.

Then we do walking meditation, weaving through the kitchen, the front hallway, turning into the living room, circling the family room.

Then we sit again.

JACK, A SOLIDLY built man in his early fifties, explains to me later, over tea, that the Downers Grove group grew out of a Chicago area retreat led in 1993 by the Vietnamese teacher Thich Nhat Hanh, the tiny, smiling monk whose book started my own interest in meditation. The retreat was simple, Jack says, like Nhat Hanh's books, and focused on walking, sitting, and mindfulness. Nhat Hanh ended the retreat by splitting the participants into small groups—based on the locations of their homes—and encouraging them to form *sanghas,* or communities of support.

Out of that retreat, Jack tells me, came a number of new sitting groups, in Chicago, throughout Illinois, in Wisconsin, and in Downers Grove. The Downers Grove group fluctuates between six and eight members, but occasionally slips back to the basic three. People filter in and out.

I ask the trio of founders why they haven't given their group a name—the Downers Grove Buddhist Society, or the Lyman Street Sangha—for more visibility.

"Well," Tom answers, "some of the people who come and sit with us are Catholic, some are nuns, and we don't want to keep anyone away. People come and sit in rocking chairs or whatever, and they know we are following Buddhist principles, but we don't make a point of it, we don't have a Buddha statue or anything."

There is a cowboy statue on an end table, and a few duck prints on the wall. That is it. None of the usual Buddhist, or even American Buddhist, symbols—no fat or skinny figurines, no wall hangings, no Asian art, no bells, no incense.

"Right, Tom acknowledges. "These are the trappings of institutionalized religion, not the basics of Buddhism itself."

Tom and Sue are also in their fifties, parents of two adult sons. It is obvious within moments of speaking to the Wolskos or to Jack

Hatfield that their regular meditation practice is a very important part of their lives, but they are quiet in their enthusiasm.

"I meditate twice a day," Jack tells me, "and I find that I have much less stress." He smiles. "I am a much better tennis player too. I think I have become much more creative at work." He is a computer consultant. "I used to be an angry person, and this practice has helped me."

Tom, a nuclear engineer working in environmental energy systems, says that meditation and Buddhist principles bring him "peace and balance. And in that peaceful state, it is amazing just how more beautiful the world really is."

Sue, petite and gray-haired, also works with computer systems. Buddhism, she says, helps her to recognize her feelings better, see them for what they are, and have more control over them. "I find myself more willing to let my friends change," she explains. "I no longer drag all the past 'garbage' of a relationship into the present and future, but let the garbage lie and take people for what they are at the moment." She still hasn't conquered anger, she admits, especially in Chicago traffic. "But I am more aware of when I might get upset, and it passes more quickly."

JACK, TOM, AND Sue, sitting in the upper-middle-class suburban family room with Catholic nuns, white-collar programmers, and all manner of folk, not bothering with even a simple Buddha statue or a stick of incense, are either on the cutting edge of American Buddhism—no Japanese spoken here, no Tibetan horns—or they are guilty of taking a deep, ancient, ethnic religion and Americanizing all the authenticity out of it. I'm sure with a few phone calls, I could find authoritative individuals to take either side of that argument. It is an ongoing controversy on the pages of *Tricycle*, in the *zendo*, in

Theravada monasteries, and among the followers of the Dalai Lama. How much of the old way is essential? How much change is good? Where does a Buddhist draw the line?

"Hey, aren't you worried that you are just watering down Buddhism?" I ask Jack. "What would you say to people who accused you of that?"

Jack shrugs. "The whole idea of watering it down is to me meaningless," he answers. "Buddhism traveled from India to China, from China to Japan, and every time it made a jump, the old guard suggested it was being watered down. But it is still here."

Sue points out that she and Tom and Jack, and the vast majority of other American Buddhists, are lay practitioners, not monks. They have kids, and jobs.

"In Japan," Tom adds, "monastics and monks are a very small part of the Buddhist population." He mentions what others, like Father Kennedy, have mentioned before—that lay practice in Japan may indeed be *less* intense than lay practice in America; people who complain that Americans aren't serious enough or disciplined enough are often engaging in a fallacy, comparing American lay people to Japanese or Tibetan monks.

"Many practitioners in Japan," Tom concludes, "are more like those Christians who only show up in Church on Easter and Christmas."

THERE IS A saying in Zen Buddhism that confounds and befuddles many a Westerner. "If you see the Buddha," the saying goes, "kill the Buddha."

Pretty brutal language for a pacifist religion, but what most people interpret the odd saying to mean is, "Even clinging to Buddhism, taking Buddhist tradition too seriously, is too much clinging, too much attachment." The Buddha himself always encouraged people to discover their own way, not just to follow his.

The Downers Grove meditators are looking for inner peace, awareness, insight—just what the Buddha sought. Can it be found in a suburban family room, surrounded by reclining chairs and cherry end tables?

Don't ask me. I've given up.

IN THE MORNING, I set out with a little Buddha statue I purchased in Atlanta sitting on my dashboard. My journey into the American Heartland seems futile now, except as evidence of how your Monkey Mind can send you all willy-nilly and waste your time.

On top of this, I'm fairly addled from too much cross-country driving and find myself talking to the carved figurine, facing him out so he can see the road. "Here little Buddha, can you see now? What the hell are we doing out here? Why didn't you tell me to stay home?"

My mother used to have a Jesus statue on the dashboard of her '59 Chevy. Dashboards were metal in those days, and Jesus was magnetized. My dash is vinyl, and my Buddha slips around wildly every time I make a turn.

I cross the Mississippi at noon, roll into Iowa City an hour or so later—I have another appointment to keep.

Soon thereafter I am stepping into the large brick building that houses the Iowa City Zen Center, and am met by a ten-foot stuffed giraffe. The first floor of the old mansion is a day care center. The *zendo* is upstairs, but no one is home.

So I take a walk. Iowa City is an idiosyncratic little college town—surrounded by farmland, but itself a miniature haven of alternative lifestyles. The small downtown has the esteemed bookstore Prairie Lights, a pagan occult shop, a New Age emporium, a shop that sells only hemp products, a few other hippie stores, all tie-dye and Grateful Dead, and seemingly everyone wears Birkenstocks. I encounter more purple hair and oddly pierced body parts per capita than I would in even New York City.

I don't realize until it is explained to me later, though, that what I am seeing is not actually Iowa City, but Iowa City, the college town, in mid-summer. Classes are in recess, I am told, and all the "normal" folks have gone home to work on the farms.

I MEET STEVE Heywood and Lynn Newman Mennenga later at the Java House, one of those nice college-town coffee shops.

Steve, a property manager, is thin, with red hair, glasses. He sips apple juice because he "has a problem with caffeine." Lynn, a forty-eight-year-old homemaker and part-time editor, is small, with short brown hair, and an easy, friendly manner. I am only half-listening, I'm afraid, as they run through the history of the Iowa City Zen Center—it started in 1969, didn't even have a name at first, and has been in flux ever since. The membership rolls wax and wane, the group will almost die out, and then it will somehow revive again.

These are nice people, they are giving me their time, and I feel ungrateful. My Project no longer makes any sense to me, but I ask the questions anyway.

About 1991, the Zen Center moved into the Willowwind Building, above the stuffed giraffe, Lynn tells me. "At that point the energy was so low we had just almost died."

I ask about current membership, and Lynn tells me that the mailing list for the group newsletter, *dharma farmer,* is 130 people, but at the average sangha meeting they only get eight to ten people showing up. "Maybe four people sit regularly," she says.

It sounds to me as if they should just give up, too—but here I am projecting again. Then Lynn reveals a surprising fact. For the first time, the Iowa City Zen Center has its own priest.

"Actually there are two," Steve points out. "Last July, the Japanese priest came, and in April or so another American priest arrived."

Taiken Yokoyama just sort of showed up in town the previous year, I am told, not invited or officially affiliated with the Zen Center. "We are not paying him," Steve explains. "He is a fifth- or sixth-generation priest from Hiroshima, and is supported by his home temple." The American, Taizan Shaeffer, was ordained in Japan, then lived in Minneapolis, and just recently came to Iowa City, where he supports himself rehabbing homes. Both men sit with the group and offer occasional instruction.

And yet another priest might be coming, Lynn tells me. Shohaku Okamura of Minnesota Zen Center, a noted translator of the works of Zen master Dogen, has mentioned once or twice that he might move to Iowa City, because he likes the small town.

"For years," Steve muses, "people have been saying, 'You know, we need to get a priest here, a teacher, and then we will really be doing Zen.' Now we have two priests here, and people are saying, 'Oh, I don't know.'"

My ears perk up—now here's a conundrum. The Iowa City Zen Center flounders, revives, stagnates, rekindles, shrinks, awakens, for nearly two decades, and then out of the blue two Zen priests arrive—and some in the congregation don't like it?

The new priests are gradually instituting more rigor, more of a schedule, more study, Lynn explains. "I think it has frightened people," she says. "One woman said to me, 'You know, I don't want this to be church. I have a lot of demands on my time, and this just seems like one more thing pulling at me.'"

I DON'T KNOW what to make of it at all. The Dalai Lama brings Tibetan practice to Bloomington, then suggests we stick to our Judeo-Christian roots. Jack and Tom and Sue form a nice, small sitting group in Downers Grove but don't even have a Buddha statue. And now the Iowa City Zen Center finds two priests and the membership is put off by all the "authenticity"? Maybe, I think, it just isn't meant to happen. Maybe my original premise—that Buddhism is fitting into America in all sorts of interesting ways, and that once I find them, I'll know something worth knowing—was wrong in the first place. Maybe it isn't fitting at all. Maybe I'm too Catholic. Maybe America is too American.

MY INTERVIEW WITH Steve and Lynn ends without my reaching any final enlightenment, but in the morning, I shuffle over to the Iowa City *zendo* for the five-thirty A.M. sitting anyway. My various Buddhist experiences have certainly changed me in one way—I get up before dawn most days, whether I need to or not.

As if to stress the paucity of my experience on this failed expedition, a bearded, portly fellow named Keith is the only one who shows up at the center that morning to join me. We sit, just the two of us, in a small room—it probably used to be a bedroom, back when this used to be a house—under an antique light fixture.

Keith isn't even sure how to work the timer, and doesn't know the ceremonial Zen chants that usually open the meditation session. He is worried about this, but I convince him I don't really care.

I don't. We just sit, and listen to the birds wake up.

And you know what? It is the nicest hour of my trip.

13

EAT YOUR RICE, WASH YOUR
BOWL, AND JUST SIT

....

Studying with the

Seven-Year-Old Master

AFTER IOWA, OF course, I could have pushed on to Kearney, Nebraska, Missoula, Montana, or Denver, Colorado, and would have found countless more stories of sincere, pleasant people struggling to fit ancient Buddhist principles into their modern American lives. And of course, heading further west, I would eventually have reached California, a state with nearly as many *zendos* as it has convenience stores.

But what would have been the point? My Project was dead.

True to my distracted, hyperactive, Monkey Mind nature, I had lurched hungrily from place to place, looking everywhere for something that wasn't to be found. One of the main lessons in Buddhism is "do not cling," and here I was, clinging like mad to a question, fully "attached" to finding some answer.

After my morning meditation at the Iowa City Zen center, I turn my car around. My little Buddha statue careens across the dash-

board, slides onto the floor, and I head back to Central Pennsylvania, which may as well be Iowa anyway, for all the corn, cows,
crows, and horses.

BUT A WEEK after my *dharma* road trip ends, there is an odd coincidence. Violating yet another of the basic precepts by craving a cold
beer, I wander into the neighborhood bottle shop, pick out a six-
pack of Yuengling, and take it to the register. Behind the counter, a
long-haired, bearded fellow sits on his stool reading *The Tibetan Book
of Living and Dying* by Sogyal Rinpoche.

"Are you a Buddhist?" I ask, surprised that anyone in my town is
reading this book, much less some fellow in a beer store.

"No," he answers sharply.

We stand looking at one another awkwardly for what is probably
only a few seconds but seems far longer, then he clears his throat
and says, "Well, yes."

"Really?"

He looks away quickly, as if ashamed or frightened, rings up my
purchase. I can only imagine what thoughts are going through his
mind. This is a very traditional rural area, overwhelmingly Christian, European-American, home to basic farm values. Central Penn-
sylvanians are simple people, by and large well-meaning, but a bit
uncomfortable with anything too new or too exotic. Perhaps he
thinks I am about to yell "witch," and the townspeople will come
with their pitchforks and burn him at the stake.

"You wanna bag for that?" he asks me.

I'm persistent, or maybe I'm a pest. "I didn't know there were any
Buddhists around here," I inquire. "Are there other Buddhists?"

Averting his eyes and mumbling somewhat, he tells me that there
is a sitting group a few miles out of town, up on Skytop Mountain,
and they meet on Monday evenings.

"Do I have to call first?"

"Nah, just show up."

IN A BEAUTIFUL mountaintop home, surrounded by trees, a pond, a small trickle of a stream, with vegetable gardens carefully fenced because of the voracious deer population, a few people sit in a large room.

There is no teacher, no formal organization or creed, but a vaguely Zen sense to things. Mainly we just sit, for a bit over an hour, broken up by some walking. Just sitting with other people is always a joy after a few weeks of sitting alone, at home.

Eventually, Len Siebert rings the bells, and Barb, his wife, arranges us in a circle to talk.

We exchange pleasantries. Everyone knows everyone else, and none of them know me, but they make me feel quite welcome. It seems as if everyone in the room—there are about eight of us—is traveling somewhere in the next month, to a retreat, or an intensive *sesshin,* or to hear some teacher. So I guess I am not alone in my Monkey-Minded wandering.

"Do you know about Diane?" someone asks me, and I admit that I do not.

"Well, she isn't far from here, and you really should meet her."

DIANE TURNS OUT to be *Dai-En,* the *dharma* name of Patricia Bennage. Dai-En Bennage, as she prefers to be called, was born and raised in Central Pennsylvania but became a professional ballerina, traveled the world, and ended up in Japan studying Zen with Omori Sogen Rotaishi. She entered Aichi Semmon Nisodo, a women's monastery, and eventually received certification as a senior teacher in the Soto Zen sect. She has also studied at Thich Nhat Hanh's Plum Village Sangha in France, and teaches in Nhat Hanh's tradition as well.

She is a highly accredited, deeply qualified Buddhist guide, and though I'm fairly burned out, a bit resistant to yet another charismatic teacher, she lives just an hour up the road. Moreover, she is a woman, and that intrigues me. From Father O' Donnell, to Brother Damien to John Daido Loori all the way to the Dalai Lama, it seems I have been seeking spirituality almost exclusively from dominant male figures. Maybe the change would be good.

The following week, I drive to Pennsdale, a small, rural town with Quaker roots. Dai-En has started the Mt. Equity Zendo in one of the more strikingly beautiful buildings I have ever seen, part of an old Quaker farmstead.

The massive farmhouse is large enough to have probably once housed four branches of the farm family. Now it is an apartment building, with nine separate units, but someone has been careful to maintain the exquisite architectural details—wide-board wood floors, rippled glass windows, classic moldings, ornate door hardware.

Dai-En rents four of the nine apartment units for her *zendo*, and on a warm summer Tuesday evening, an even dozen of us sit on the beige carpet of one of the small downstairs rooms.

We introduce ourselves—two physicians, a nurse, a medical receptionist, two psychologists, an artist, a craftsman, two teachers, a student, and me. No matter what happens to me this evening, my Monkey Mind jokes to itself, there is surely someone in the room that can deal with it.

A small woman with a beaming face, Dai-En nearly disappears into a ball when she leans over to do her full prostration bow. Her head is shaved, and someone tells me that when she first returned to her hometown, people were gracious and consoling—they mistakenly thought that she had cancer, and that the chemotherapy had caused her to go bald.

The shaved heads are for simplicity's sake, actually. One less attachment, one less chore to distract one from one's meditative practice.

We chant, sit for about thirty minutes, walk, then sit some more. You know the drill by now as well as I do. The windows are thrown open for air circulation. Outside I see fireflies. I can hear the catbirds. I have given up grasping for anything, and as any good Buddhist could tell you, I'm suddenly finding it all the more accessible.

DAI-EN, IT TURNS out, is in Pennsdale to be closer to her eighty-year-old mother, Evelyn, who also lives in the apartment building. Evelyn Bennage doesn't join us for the meditation, but she comes in later to talk. She is a spry, spunky woman with a lovely twinkle in her eye, and she has recently taken the precepts.

"My mother came over one day and said, 'I guess someone like me can't do it,'" Dai-En explains, turning to take a short, fond look at her mom, "but I said 'Yes, of course, you already do so much to support the work that goes on here, it would only be fair.'"

Though not much inclined to the rigors of long sitting meditation, Evelyn helps to wash and iron the various ritual cloths, shops for the food, and makes the tea, and her apartment kitchen serves as the *zendo* kitchen when large groups come in. Dai-En came up with a shortened version of the Buddhist precepts, suitable for someone so old and not ready to take on too much, and Evelyn now has the *dharma* name Raku-En.

"What do your friends think?" I ask Dai-En's mother.

"Oh, at the senior citizens center, saying 'Buddha' is like dropping a bomb," she laughs, then gives me a wink. "So I don't say it."

I like Evelyn Raku-En Bennage immediately, and figure she probably most resembles the sort of Buddhist I can become. A Buddhist with one eye winking. I'm not I sure I believe, though, that she doesn't tell her senior citizen pals what she is up to. Evelyn has the delightful air of a woman who might like to drop a bomb on the old-timers once in a while, just to get a little rise out of them.

I CONTINUE RATHER uneven contact with the people up on Skytop Mountain, my local sitting group. They remain gentle and welcoming. More often, I sit alone in my living room, or in my garden with all the bugs and birds, my little sentient teachers.

Late in August, I return to Mt. Equity Zendo for a Day of Mindfulness, a program Dai-En offers based on Thich Nhat Hanh's books and teachings. His words are part of what started me on this journey, so I am especially interested to see what the Mindfulness practice might entail.

We meditate for a very short period on our cushions, keeping it relaxed for the newcomers, then do walking meditation inside, and then, wonder of wonders, we do walking meditation outside, on the old Quaker farm, on a beautiful, low-humidity Sunday morning, in the warm summer sun.

The walking meditation I have done previously has been focused primarily on stretching out the leg muscles—you keep the meditative center inside, and only interact with the outside world enough to keep from plowing into the meditator in front of you. In the Nhat Hanh tradition, however, you interact as much as you want. The idea is to stop if you see a flower, stop if you see a cobweb, stop and look at the bark of the elm tree, the moss, the ants climbing up the side. It is not dissimilar to the 'deep looking' technique I had discovered in my garden, on those days when I was searching for the truant ladybugs.

Without this Mindfulness technique, what Nhat Hanh calls "being in the present moment," most of us tend to rush through our side yards only as a way to get to the car, and we never see the wonderful, or at least interesting, things that are right under our nose. I've witnessed people who hike through the woods in this way—so intent on finishing the hardy forest excursion, they barely experience it.

Worse still, many of us live our entire lives in this manner. We race through what is happening right now—barely noticing our families, our friends, our relationships, the natural world that surrounds us—thinking only of the job advancement to come, or of the day we pay off that debt, or of some sort of future reward or recognition, whatever it is we imagine will make us ultimately happy. We might as well be dead, we are missing so much.

In the worst-case scenario, we squander forty-five good years of life looking narrowly forward to retirement. And then what? We harbor our regrets.

Focus on being happy now, right where you are, Nhat Hanh urges us, rather than always putting it off for some indefinite future.

There is an old West African proverb, "Why tell animals living in the water to drink?" Well, animals are smarter than humans, or at least it seems so sometimes. We humans live in the water that is our life, yet we complain of constant thirst.

SO ANYWAY, WALKING on the old Quaker land, following Daien's tiny footsteps, I notice many things—squiggling insect larvae in a water barrel, a giant oak tree whose roots threaten to lift and destroy the farmstead's old icehouse, flowering weeds more intricate than any of the costly perennials I grow at home, mourning doves, crystal blue sky, cheerful white clouds.

Then we go back inside, chant a little, meditate for a short while, and have lunch on the floor—tomato sandwiches, rice cakes and cheese, pita bread and hummus. Dai-En quietly asks that we eat the meal as if it were our last meal, which seems a bit gruesome, but that is what mindfulness is all about. Enjoy it *now*. Taste your food.

Buddhists focus quite a bit on impermanence, and some outsiders see this as dismal. But face it, we *will* all ultimately die—there is just no way around it, no matter how rich or how smart you can become—and acknowledging this simple truth, Buddhists believe, will make us more free, more able to enjoy the life we do have.

Dai-En knows a bit about impermanence and last meals.

She teaches Zen to prisoners at the federal penitentiary in nearby Lewisburg, and some of her students are on death row. When she speaks of the inmates, male and female, that she has met, or when she refers to her students, many of whom are drawn to study Buddhism because of cancer, or divorce, or some tragedy that has upset the apple cart of their lives— too often it takes a tragedy to make us pay attention, doesn't it?—she isn't speaking abstractly of pain and suffering, or referring to them as examples of *dukkha,* discontent. She is sincerely troubled, genuinely pained by their anguish.

Compassion is not a concept when Dai-En speaks. You can feel it coming off of her; it is something in the way she looks at her students. She doesn't just sit on her cushion and lecture us about relieving suffering—she wants it to happen. She has, it seems, a personal stake. Maybe this is just Dai-En Bennage's nature, or perhaps it is a sign of the feminine in the teacher.

Dai-En also manages, in her meditation instructions, in her *dharma* talks, in her way of fielding questions and asking the entire group to come up with answers, to project the sense that we are practicing *with* her, alongside her, sharing *her* struggle to live up to the Zen rigors and the Thich Nhat Hanh–based awareness. The male teachers I have encountered, even those like Bhante G. and Geshe-la who openly admitted their own flaws and imperfection, somehow give the impression that we are not so much practicing alongside them, but rather practicing to become them.

Many teachers, it seems to me, cultivate the sense that "I am here, so if you want the difficult teachings come and get them, but if not, then go on along." Zen, in fact, has a tradition of throwing new students out the front door.

Dai-En strikes a different chord, and makes me want to try a little harder because she makes me imagine it actually matters to her whether or not I succeed.

One of her last bits of advice, before the six-hour mindfulness retreat ends and we return to our busy realities, is that we should try to practice in a way that invites our family in, rather than excluding them. "A practice that excludes family can be very dangerous," she warns, and I think about the trouble she has gone through herself—moving to rural Pennsdale just to be near her mother, an area with so few Buddhist devotees that simply meeting the rent and paying the phone bill is a daunting chore, and then finding a way to bring her mother into the practice—and I figure that maybe I should be including my own family more.

I have been seeing them as an impediment, as a series of interruptions, and have focused on trying to meditate when they were out of the house. I see now, however, that if I can devote hours to finally noticing all the bugs and birds in my yard, then surely I can work harder to notice my wife and daughter.

DURING THE TIME that I have been visiting monasteries and attending retreats, my wife, Renita, has been worshipping with the Quakers, and she shows little interest in converting to Buddhism. It isn't the concepts that bother her—she is very open to odd, new ideas—it is her knees. After years of earning her living as a professional modern dancer, her joints don't flex the way mine do. There is no way she will ever willingly settle down on a *zafu* for hours.

But Quakers and Buddhists, we have discovered, share more than a few key concepts: the importance of simplicity, the wisdom of looking inside, the focus on peace and nonviolent means. Renita and I exchange notes on the sofa many evenings and find ourselves saying, "It's the same thing, just different words," over and over again. While Buddhists rummage through layers of mind weeds searching for the ground of being, Quakers sit in quiet contemplation, listening for a "still small voice within." For Quakers, that voice is a message from God. For Buddhists, it is our true nature speaking. I am unsure if the distinction is theological or semantic. Thich Nhat Hanh prods us to live our lives in mindfulness; Quakers are encouraged to "walk in the light." And just like a fully realized Buddha is obligated to come down off the mountain into the world and help others achieve enlightenment, Quakerism is more than just a set of beliefs, it is a call to social action.

It turns out, in fact, that I might conceivably have learned some of this same philosophy at a place like Good Shepherd, or from Brother Damien perhaps, if I had stayed around my old religion long enough. While I'm looking into Buddhism, contemplative prayer, a thousand-year-old practice with links to the twentieth-century Trappist monk and writer Thomas Merton, is experiencing a resurgence among Catholics. Thomas Keating, a Trappist monk and one of the leaders of the new Catholic contemplative movement, explains his belief that God is "closer than breathing, closer than consciousness itself. You can't get away from Him even if you wanted to, and it is only in your thoughts that you are not united with Him."

Our very thoughts get in the way, the busy noise of the world keeps us separate from the divine, Keating says, so he urges Catholics to "stop thinking" and intentionally give themselves over to the spiritual messages inside. Even Trappists can become enlightened.

But Catholics *and* Quakers believe in Jesus, while Buddhists—well nowadays, it all depends on whom you ask. There is no Jesus in traditional Asian Buddhism, obviously, but teachers like Thich Nhat Hanh see no problem with integrating Jesus' teachings into the *dharma*. Even John Daido Loori, who, as an Italian-American kid from New Jersey, was probably himself raised a Catholic, sometimes quotes the Gospel. Father Kennedy is a Zen teacher and a Jesuit, a fact that still surprises me.

Because Buddhists don't talk much about God, they are sometimes mistakenly labeled atheists. Some Buddhists maintain that the question of God is really secondary—we have to know ourselves first, and that can take a lifetime. Others say that the Buddhist concept of enlightenment, the realization that we are all one and must help one another, is not so different from what Christians call the "state of grace."

Whether or not Buddhists believe in God comes down, probably, to a matter of definition. Is God a distinct being, a creator up in heaven somewhere, this big Michelangelo figure with rippling muscles and a white beard, always holding a stone tablet? Many of us were raised to believe that; Buddhists certainly are not. Or is God an energy, a force, an invisible glue that holds us together?

"God is Love," the nuns used to say.

Well, Buddhists would have no problem with that.

IMAGINING THAT PERHAPS we aren't so far apart after all, Renita and I strike a compromise—in the mornings, after our daughter Maria gets on her yellow school bus, we do *zazen* together for twenty minutes. I rest on my *zafu*, my legs growing numb. Renita either sits on the sofa or reclines on her back. I chase my Monkey

Mind from limb to slippery limb. Renita prays and thinks her Quaker thoughts.

It is very nice.

Buddhism. Mindfulness. Contemplative prayer. It doesn't really matter what you call it. We both seem calmer the remainder of the day.

MARIA, OUR SEVEN-year-old, insists that she is "not a Quaker," but usually says this only when she doesn't feel like getting dressed for Quaker First Day School.

She also makes it very clear that she thinks Buddhism is silly. I buy her a picture book, *Rahula Leads the Way*, in which a little boy in monk's garb with a shaved head leads another little boy named Leo in adventures of mindfulness and compassion—sharing a picnic, noticing a waterfall, overcoming anger, caring for a baby bird.

One night I read the book to Maria, and on the final page, Rahula says, "We haven't finished our journey yet. The path is long and in some places difficult. But we'll make many new friends along the way who will help us and keep us company."

Hoping to engage my daughter in some philosophical speculation, I put the book aside and ask, "Where do you suppose he is going?"

"Who?"

"Rahula. Where do you think he might be headed?"

"I don't know." She shrugs and grins. "The bathroom?"

RAHULA HAS BEEN traveling the countryside all day, so Maria's answer makes a certain kind of conspicuous sense. Zen teachers through the centuries have repeatedly reminded students that Buddhism should not become too complicated.

Take this famous *koan*, for example:

A monk asks the teacher Chao-chou, "I have just entered this monastery. Please teach me."

Chao-chou asks, "Have you eaten your rice?"

The monk says, "Yes."

Chao-chou says, "Then go wash your bowl."

The monk is enlightened.

Eat your rice. Wash your bowl. Then maybe go to the bathroom. What could be more mindful? Perhaps my daughter is a Zen master, and just doesn't know it.

DESPITE MARIA'S RESISTANCE, or maybe amusement is the better word, I resolve to keep the focus at home.

After all my travels, my retreats, my experiences with Daido-shi and the Dalai Lama, my bouncing from *zendo* to *zendo*, meditation group to meditation group, and my repeated attempts to make my own daily sitting practice rigid and noble, one thing is clear—I'm never going to live in a monastery, become Tibetan, or master the many nuances of Asian ritual. I was never much of an altar boy. In fact, I was only on the altar once, for my sister Sally's wedding, and Father O' Donnell was so unimpressed by my performance, he instructed the nuns to find me something else to do.

I am a writer and a teacher, a secular fellow who likes to eat and to joke. I have a wife and a daughter, and I live in the midst of our massively complex contemporary society. Though I can do it occasionally on retreat, I surely will never find a way to sit regularly for four hours a day.

And I am probably missing the forest for the trees anyway. I have too many traditions. Too many teachers. Too many books. Too many concepts bouncing around my brain. Too many Buddhisms vying for my attention.

"Just sit," John Daido Loori told me way back at my first retreat.

"Just look," Thich Nhat Hanh is telling me now. "Just look, and see what is right before you."

"Practice *with* your family," Dai-En urges. Don't close the door and go away.

"Eat your rice, wash your bowl," Chao-chou reminds me.

I AM GLAD there are people who devote their lives to monastic practice, and others who study ancient Pali dialects so they might memorize every word written about the ancient Buddha, but as for myself, I'm sure now that if I'm going to have a Buddhist practice, that practice will have to be woven into my life, not constructed apart from it.

My family is my *sangha*, as are my students, my friends, my tennis partner Bruce, Barbara and Len up on Skytop Mountain, the squirrels and birds in my yard, that guy in the beer store, and when I manage to schedule a retreat, all those other American Buddhist seekers. It is good to understand impermanence, nonattachment, the Eightfold Path to Enlightenment, and the many laws of *karma*, but these can become mind weeds, too.

If you see the Buddha, kill the Buddha. If it all becomes too cerebral, run out into the yard, waggle your tongue, and chase the squirrels.

AND FINALLY, AS if to underscore all of this, my daughter Maria teaches me one more lesson in her unpretentious, childlike Zen.

One evening, we are wrestling on the sofa, fighting for the television remote control, and she calls me Stupid Dad.

I have been reading Buddhism books all day, so in my parental pedantic way, I respond by trying to sneak in a thinly veiled lesson on nonduality.

"How can I be stupid?" I ask her. "When there is no me, no self, no one there to be stupid. We are all one thing, you know. So if I am stupid, then you are stupid."

Zen master Maria thinks a moment, then whacks her student on the head with a stuffed tiger.

"Dad," she says, "that's *really* stupid."

14

WHAT KIND OF
BUDDHIST AM I?

A Lousy One, Thank You

BUDDHISM IS ALIVE with contradictions, and I am as well. After my realization that I am not cut out for monasticism, or for any particularly rigorous form of Buddhism, and that visiting all of these retreats and teachers was pure Monkey Mind in and of itself, I return to Zen Mountain Monastery anyway, hauling my duffle bag through the front door one more time.

My first visit to John Daido Loori's big house on the hill is only a year in the past, but it seems like forever. I come because I am curious to know some things about myself—even if my frantic seeking was ill-advised, did my practice deepen any as a result? Can I sit with more stillness? Has the smallness of mind that led me to obsess about my snoring roommate gone away?

The autumn *sesshin* is an intensive period of meditation during which no one speaks and even eye contact is forbidden. We sit in meditation from five in the morning until nine in the evening, with only brief breaks for work practice, leg stretching, and meals. A week-long *sesshin* involves nearly one hundred hours of sitting meditation, a real test of one's mettle. Based on my limited previous experience, I am told to come for just the final four days.

They put me on a cushion right off. Most of the faces are the same—Jimon is *zendo* monitor, keeping everybody in line and on time—but for me, the experience is far different. I am not looking around so much, because there is not so much to look at. We are just sitting there. I am not thinking about my roommates because I don't know anything about them—we aren't allowed to talk, or even smile at one another. Some of the rigmarole is still present, the bells, the drums, the chanting, the incense, but they don't distract me so much. I don't particularly feel drawn to them, but I don't particularly care. I skip *dokusan* altogether.

What I find is that I truly like the long hours of sitting. Sure, there are occasional moments where I think I might scream and flee the building because of my inability to concentrate, because of the mind's tendency to want to run away from stillness, but these are balanced by instances of sheer bliss, moments where my constantly agitated, routinely dissatisfied intellect is finally able to relax. As the days progress, my brain begins to feel the way one's muscles feel after a really good, really deep massage.

Though I have understood up until now the idea of quieting the brain so as to reach some new level of understanding, it has mostly been theory. On the cushion, on the third day, it becomes real. The mind is like a bowl of water, I realize, sloshing back and forth, spilling out the sides. Most of us have lives like earthquakes, so the water is in constant motion. Add to this the fact that we are always grabbing at the water, struggling to make sense of our brain messages, yet all the grabbing just further churns the liquid. Two things have to happen for the bowl of water to come to rest. First you have to turn off the faucet, stop all the input. Second, you have to quit grabbing.

The silent retreat, the lack of even eye contact, is designed to stop the faucet. It is up to the individual, on the cushion, to stop the grabbing, if he can.

What happens finally, if you are successful, is that the water settles, and Buddhist masters will tell you that the still water of the mind then becomes a mirror, in which you can find yourself.

Well, my water never fully settles. I guess it would have taken more than four days, and why not, I've been churning it for forty years. But it settles down enough for me to see glimpses of the calm center, to know that the calm center is there. In fact, what is most striking to me is just seeing for myself how much stuff there really is whisking around inside my brain, and how much remains even after all that silent meditation. And though the stuff still whirls around some, it slows enough that I can actually identify what I see. For once in my life, it is not all a blur.

You don't need to be a Buddhist to do what we did at the Zen Mountain *sesshin*. You simply need to be someone who turns off the television, shuts off the distractions, ignores the phone, and just sits, listening to the signals of the mind. Buddhism can help, though. At least among fellow Buddhists, people won't think you are nuts.

And you can't do it in half an hour. I couldn't even do it in four days. You can't slow the brain down with a few brief attempts any more easily than you can stop a speeding freight train with a white picket fence.

But it can be done. I saw that.

JOHN DAIDO LOORI showed himself at brief intervals, mainly as he ducked in and out of the *dokusan* room, and he spoke to us on the final day. Daido-shi had both intrigued me and raised my suspicions during my first Zen Mountain experience—too much of the practice, I thought, was centered on meeting the "Living Buddha." Or perhaps it was my own wish to know him, impress him, find his favor, that bothered me. At Change Your Mind Day in Central Park that hot afternoon, he was engaging, funny, and a bit more human, but occasionally condescending. Of course, the questions from the audience hadn't given him much to work with.

Perhaps Daido-shi saves his more sincere, thoughtful side for more serious events, or perhaps I am now more receptive, but the abbot seems genuine, humble, and honest during the discussions that end the *sesshin*. He isn't acting the guru, he is acting the teacher. He is at the front of the room because he has been at this longer than any of us, and he knows a few things that might help. And if he has charisma, if we are drawn to him, it is because he seems so damn happy with what he has learned.

Buddhism is at no loss for metaphors, and Daido-shi gives me one more to work with. He says the problem with all of us, the reason we live in vague discontent and constant yearning, is that we carry around a ball and chain.

"Before we are born, we have an itsy-bitsy ball and chain," he explains. "You know, I like it better when Mom plays Mozart. I like it better when this thick watery world I live in moves around less. Then we are born, and that little ball and chain gets bigger and bigger and bigger."

We begin to prefer things, and we want those preferences to continue. We become insistent that things be just as we want them to be, all the time. I like it better when my mom talks to me and not the other children. I like it better when I am the most popular kid in school. I like it better when I earn more money than my neighbor. I like it better when my wife always smiles. The more we insist on our preferences, the bigger our ball and chain, and the more it weighs us down.

But if we don't prefer things, then we increase our chances to be content. We don't have to like a rainy day, or a wet, cold, slushy December afternoon, necessarily, we just have to take it, notice it, and pass through it, without dwelling on our preference that it be different. We don't have to wait for the sun to come out, either, before we can be happy. We can be happy every day.

We stop ourselves from contentment, from peace, in other words, and then blame the rest of the world. Buddhism says look at yourself, take the blame, and change it.

ON THE FINAL afternoon of *sesshin*, we are allowed to speak. I attempt to tell the group how much I have realized but end up just babbling.

The fellow I have been sitting next to for four days, a nice young man who might himself have been a Catholic once, turns to me and says, "It was a pleasure sitting beside you. You sit like a rock."

His name isn't Damien, it is Patrick, but it seems more than coincidence that he echoes the Catholic monk's words from so long ago. I have completed a circle.

IT WASN'T UNTIL I gave up on my questions, until I abandoned my Project, that I began to see real answers. Ironic, but it makes a certain sort of sense. Buddhism tends to be slippery, like the wet, frightened sunfish I pulled out of Lake Erie as a boy. The basic concepts shine and flash, then glide right through your fingers. The only way to hold a sunfish is not to hold it too hard.

I didn't find what I was looking for—some heart of American Buddhism, some truth about how it will eventually find a comfortable fit with our modern Western lives—but on a personal level, I found more than I ever anticipated, felt more than I am probably willing to admit. Though I can't pull Buddhism out of my back pocket and show it to you now, I think the basics of the teaching are not so obscure. *Be kind, be careful, be yourself. Think before you act. Love your neighbor. Pay attention. If you are miserable, look in the mirror to find out why.*

I also learned that my lingering dissatisfaction, my gloom, that rock inside of me, the end product of my adolescent anger, is nothing so unique. It is *dukkha,* that old ball and chain.

AM I ENLIGHTENED?

Hardly.

Or depending on how you define it, maybe.

If enlightenment is a thunderbolt to the forehead, an instantaneous, life-transforming event, an explosion of pure insight that forever changes you, then not only have I missed it, but it would be silly of me to even expect it in such a short amount of time, especially given my inclination to giggle under my breath.

But some Buddhists suggest that enlightenment is a gradual process, that it arrives one step at a time, beginning with the first momentary experience of *samadhi* and deepening thereafter, indefinitely. Well, I experienced something like *samadhi* more than once—on my cushion, at Zen Mountain Monastery, in West Virginia, at home, in my garden—and though I am not greatly altered, I am certainly not the same.

If enlightenment is gradual, then yes, I have experienced a smidgen of enlightenment, and I am happy for it. You must take me at my word, I suppose, but the truth is, there are more mornings when I wake up looking forward to the day, and more evenings when I go to bed thinking, Well, not a bad few hours.

• • •

CAN BUDDHISM EVENTUALLY fit into mainstream America? Is it taking solid root? Is it a significant national spiritual movement, or just our passing fancy?

Well, the numbers are small, perhaps, but the adherents I found in states like West Virginia, North Carolina, Iowa, and Indiana— throughout the country really—are sincere. These people aren't just kidding around. They are working at it. They sit, they think, they study, they try to better the world around them.

On the other hand, America is not about to be swallowed by Asian thought, and the Judeo-Christian religious leaders of our nation need not rise in panic.

No one seems sure how many practicing Buddhists exist here in the United States. One reason is that you can practice Buddhism at home, on your cushion, just sitting, breathing, and harnessing your mental attachments, signed on to no formal church roster. So how will you be counted? It probably goes against Buddhist philosophy to even try to count.

And no central Buddhist Council of Churches or American Buddhist Synod exists. Temples, monasteries, *zendos,* and retreat centers—an estimated 1,500 of them scattered across the fifty states—by and large operate independently of one another. Even Buddhist groups of the same basic sect, Zen Centers for instance, operate under no central authority, so no one is running around with statistics in hand.

Those who have attempted rough estimates of Buddhists in this country put the number between one and three million people. Not an overwhelming total, but still, that's a lot of sentient beings.

American Buddhism is small, and may remain so. Buddhists are not proselytizers, and nonduality teaches that the numbers don't matter anyway. If you are a Buddhist, then so is everyone else. And of course, the Tibetans might remind you to also count the blue jays, squirrels, and ladybugs. They may also be Buddhists, living through one of their more adventurous incarnations.

LESS IMPORTANT THAN quantity, surely, is quality.

Is Buddhism diluted, degraded, cheapened by our American ways? Are we talking about real Buddhism here, or something easier to swallow, maybe Buddhism Lite?

Overall, I tend to think this American Buddhism is real. Of course, I can give you spurious examples—Steven Seagal's sadistic Buddhist movie heroes, the "Hello, Dalai" Danka fax commercial, the rock concert approach to enlightenment—but what other world religion hasn't been similarly mocked by our popular culture excesses?

We have nowhere near the tradition of monasticism and devotion in this country that is found in, say, Japan, but those who *are* devoting themselves to the Buddhist life seem to be devoting themselves with real rigor. Life is no picnic at a Zen Mountain Monastery *sesshin*. Bhante Dhamma and Bhante Rahula, helping Bhante G. carve the Bhavana Society out of the West Virginia woods, are certainly not taking the easy way out.

And remember, most Buddhists in America will remain lay Buddhists, just as the vast majority of Buddhists in Asian countries do not live in monasteries, do not meditate daily, have not memorized the sacred Pali texts.

When I was at Mt. Equity Zendo doing the Mindfulness Day with Dai-En Bennage, a Japanese gentleman spoke briefly during our self-introductions about his own search for the *dharma*. "Growing up in Japan," he said in his soft, heavily accented English, "I had no real idea what Buddhism was about. The priests would come to the house and chant the sutras, but they would chant them in Chinese. My father would give the priests some money, and they would go on to the next house. That is all I knew."

Now that he is here in the United States, the man tells us, he is curious about the faith of his ancestors, and finally ready to study.

"Imagine," he laughs, "coming to America to find out about Buddhism."

WELL, WHY NOT?

If what the Buddha taught is true, then it is as true in Arkansas as it is in Tibet.

And frankly, Buddhism has as many problems in its countries of origin as it has here. Though 78 percent of Japanese people profess to be Buddhist, newspapers report that changing social attitudes and urban life are threatening the continued existence of rural Japanese monasteries and of the priestly lineage. The average Japanese Buddhist, the experts will tell you, is just not that interested.

For those who complain that Buddhism is shallow in America, let me tell you a story. For most Japanese people, Buddhism doesn't come into play every day, or even every Sunday morning. For many, it becomes an issue only on occasions like weddings and funerals. Well, the demand for priest-led rituals at Yokohama Central Cemetery became so great a few years back that Zen monk Hirato Isao invented an amazingly lifelike, Disneyesque robot, dubbed Robopriest, to fill the bill.

"He is well versed in the liturgy of ten Japanese Buddhist sects," Isao explains, "and, when he chants the sutras, his lips and facial muscles move in time to the prerecorded blessings. Most real human priests are not half as diligent as him. They turn up late, rush through the morning service, leaving half of it out, then drive off to play golf."

Many Japanese, it has been reported, actually prefer the robot, and ask for him by name.

• • •

ARE AMERICANS CHANGING Buddhism to fit their culture?

Probably not enough, yet.

One drawback, to my mind, of maintaining the Asian ritual, customs, and language when we teach Buddhism in the West is the danger of mistaking the trappings for the truth. The ability to throw around foreign terminology, chant in a strange tongue, and wear odd-looking clothes does not make one more fully awake to the true nature of human existence.

"Eventually," the Dalai Lama has predicted, "through a kind of evolution and without changing the essence, there will truly develop a British Buddhism, or an American Buddhism, or a French Buddhism. This is not only possible, but necessary, because this allows the essence of Buddhism to be more easily available to individuals in these cultures."

Well, far be it from me to contradict a reincarnate King.

SO WHAT KIND of a Buddhist am I? Zen, Tibetan, Theravada, American?

I don't know. It doesn't matter.

In the future, I will sit whenever possible, as much as possible, missing days here and there surely, and will continue on occasion to read about Buddhism, but my real practice will be found in how I relate to my daughter, how I handle myself in traffic, and the way I look at things. I will no doubt break the precepts left and right, slip into my old patterns, prefer foods that do me no good, and find myself all tangled up in my own thoughts often enough. But at least now I know there is an alternative.

What kind of Buddhist am I?

I think I am probably a fairly lousy Buddhist.

But Buddhism, thankfully, is a tradition with plenty of room, even for lousy Buddhists.

MAYBE MY PROJECT failed, maybe I didn't find the big answers, but you know what? I feel clearer. I feel calmer. I feel good. People around me, both family, close friends, and some folks who see me only at the office, have remarked on my new composure. "How do you stay so calm?" they ask. I just shrug.

Another change, though it very much embarrasses the skeptic inside of me to say so, is that my belief in a God has honestly been strengthened. I feel like there must be a God, because I see evidence of God everywhere—in people, in flowers, in the trees, the insects, and yes, even in myself. (Believe me, that's something new.)

"We had all these children, and all these nuns trying to teach all these children, and we simplified, we simplified God into a lovable simple commodity," Father Kennedy told me that morning in Jersey City.

He was right on the money. My growing away from religion, from God, from faith, had a lot to do with that cartoon figure Sister Mary Catherine drew on the blackboard. Just like all kids eventually figure out that no fat man in a red suit could ever fit down a chimney, it finally became clear to me one day that God didn't sit in the sky, behind the clouds, and that he wasn't going to personally intervene at key moments to save me from distress. When that simple, visible, tangible God went away, I wasn't left with much of anything but the guilt.

Buddhism didn't give me a new God, but it gave me a new way to think about God, and I guess it gave me a way to slow down enough to actually feel something.

In the end, I still have the same reluctance to take things on faith. I can't say for sure that there is a God, but neither can I rationally prove that there is not. So I'm not going to worry about it. If there is a God, I should live my life according to principles of kindness, compassion, and awareness, and if there is no God, well then I should live my life according to principles of kindness, compassion, and awareness anyway.

How wonderfully simple.

How Buddhist.

BASIC BUDDHIST TERMS

....

BUDDHISTS REVEL IN contradictions, and defining particular words in Buddhism can be like trying to pick up a wet bar of soap
in the shower. The firmer you try to grasp the meaning of the term,
the more it shoots out of your hand and caroms around the stall.

Nonetheless, here are some simple definitions for some basic Buddhist words.

Bhante
The honorific given a male teacher in Theravada Buddhism.

bodhisattva
One who, upon achieving his or her own enlightenment, delays
passing on into *nirvana,* selflessly choosing instead to stick around
the mundane Earthly plane and help others achieve their own enlightenment.

Buddha

Enlightened one, or one who is awake. Those of us who took a Varieties of Religious Experience course in college probably learned about Siddhartha Gautama, sometimes called Gautama Siddhartha, and also known as Shakyamuni Buddha. He is the *historical* Buddha, the fellow who founded the religion around 500 B.C. But in fact there are numerous other Buddhas—anyone who has achieved enlightenment subsequent to Siddartha is also a Buddha. Some even believe that there were Buddhas, or Enlightened Ones, prior to Siddhartha—cavemen Buddhas—though we don't know who they were. There may be a Buddha living down the street from you. She may or may not be a practicing Buddhist—it is not really a requirement.

dharma

Loosely translated, phenomena, or any element of existence. *Dharma* is one of the hardest terms to define, because it seems to mean anything and everything. It also refers to the nature of reality, the underlying structure of the universe. Finally, *dharma* is used to refer to the Buddha's teachings, as in "study the *dharma* and you will be enlightened."

dokusan

In Zen Buddhism, face-to-face teaching, a highly ritualized encounter between a student and a teacher. It is in *dokusan* that students are often presented with *koans* to chew over.

dukkha

Pain, suffering, or dissatisfaction. Why do we never feel fulfilled? Why does gaining something pleasurable—money, career recognition, love—just make us crave more? This craving is *dukkha,* and Buddhism aims to end it.

duality

Humans tend to imagine that everything is separate—we are separate from other people, from plants, from the moon, from the stars. This sense of duality—of there being an "us" and a "them"—is seen as the root of all *dukkha*. Buddhists believe in nonduality. If we are all one thing, then there is no sense in desiring more.

enlightenment

Though cartoon Zen illustrates this as a sudden lightbulb of realization, most Buddhists will tell you that enlightenment is a gradual understanding of where the individual fits into the world and how the individual can achieve peace.

Four Noble Truths

The basis of the Buddha's teachings on why so many of us are so dissatisfied when we have so much. The four truths are:

1. Life is *dukkha*.
2. The cause of *dukkha* is our desire.
3. It is possible, however, to end this desire.
4. The way to end it is through the Eightfold Path: right views, right aim, right speech, right action, right living, right effort, right mindfulness, right concentration.

gassho

The gesture of bringing one's hands together, palm to palm. It is often accompanied by a bow from the waist.

Gautama

See **Buddha**.

Geshe

A title given to Tibetan Buddhists who have undergone a rigorous course of study. Sort of a Doctorate in Tibetan Philosophy.

karma

The Buddhist law of cause and effect. Your *karma*, good or bad, is not random, but rather is a direct result of your past actions. See Chapter Seven for more details.

kesa

A monk's outer robe.

kinhin

Walking meditation, used both as an exercise in focused concentration and to stretch the legs after long intervals of *zazen*.

koan

Not really a riddle, though they certainly seem like riddles. *Koans* are "cases" or "stories" that illustrate some basic concept of Zen Buddhism. Focused concentration on individual *koans* is one path to enlightenment, but don't try to solve them logically.

kuti

A one-room hut. These are the primary residences for monks and nuns at the Bhavana Society, a Theravada meditation center.

kyosaku stick

A long, flat stick used by meditation hall monitors to whack the shoulders of sitting meditators, usually, but not always, at their request. Long hours of sitting meditation can lead to tense shoulders.

mala

A bracelet with wooden beads, common among Tibetan Buddhists.

nirvana

Not a place, but a mental state where craving and suffering have been totally extinguished.

nonduality

"I am he as you are he as you are me and we are all together"— John Lennon and Paul McCartney. See **duality.**

prajna

Wisdom.

samadhi

A state of focused concentration, free from all goals and distractions. *Samadhi* is usually reached only through long hours of often frustrating meditation.

samsara

Longing, or *dukkha.* If you spend so much time obsessing over past mistakes and future worries that you miss the flowers blooming right outside your window, you are locked in a cycle of *samsara.*

sangha

A Buddhist spiritual community. If you sit *zazen* at the East Poughkeepsie Zendo, then the others who sit there are your *sangha.* Alternately, since all beings are said to have an essential Buddha-nature, *sangha* refers to everyone, including the bugs and the trees.

satori

An experience of enlightenment, which is sometimes only momentary.

seiza bench

A low, angled wooden bench used in place of a *zafu* for sitting meditation.

sensei

In Zen, a title meaning "teacher."

sentient being

Anyone, anything that is capable of feeling. See Chapter 10.

sesshin

A period of intense practice, marked by long hours of sitting and total silence.

Shakyamuni

See **Buddha.**

Siddhartha

See **Buddha.**

Soto Zen

One of the two main traditions in Japanese Zen. Soto Zen stresses "sitting" while the Rinzai school often puts more emphasis on *koan* work, but in fact both schools utilize both methods.

Theravada Buddhism

The Way of the Elders. The oldest form of Buddhism, found primarily in Sri Lanka, Thailand, Burma, and Southeast Asia.

Tibetan Buddhism
A relatively new form of Buddhism, highly structured and centered in Tibet. The Dalai Lama heads up the Gelugpa tradition within Tibetan Buddhism, and was the secular ruler of Tibet as well before the 1959 invasion by China.

zafu
A pillow used in sitting meditation to help keep a straight spine. They are most often round and black, especially in Zen Buddhism.

zazen
Sitting meditation.

Zen Buddhism
An "innovative" form of Mahayana Buddhism. Mahayana spread from India into China, Korea, and Japan. Relations between the Mahayanists and the Theravadans have not always been pleasant. Zen represents only one school within the Buddhist tradition, but it is the school with which most Westerners are most familiar.

zendo
A meditation hall.

SUGGESTED FURTHER READING

....

INTERESTED IN PURSUING your own enlightenment? These books can get you started.

Gunaratana, Henepola. *Mindfulness in Plain English* (Boston: Wisdom Publications, 1992).

Kabat-Zinn, Jon. *Wherever You Go, There You Are* (New York: Hyperion, 1994).

Kamenetz, Rodger. *The Jew in the Lotus* (San Francisco: Harper Collins, 1994).

Kennedy, Robert Jinsen. *Zen Spirit, Christian Spirit* (New York: Continuum, 1995).

Loori, John Daido. *The Eight Gates of Zen* (Mt. Tremper, N.Y.: Dharma Communications, 1992).

Nhat Hanh, Thich. *The Miracle of Mindfulness* (Boston: Beacon Press, 1987).

Nhat Hanh, Thich. *Being Peace* (Berkeley, Calif.: Parallax Press, 1987).

Sahn, Seung. *Dropping Ashes on the Buddha* (New York: Grove Press, 1976).

Suzuki, Shunryu. *Zen Mind, Beginner's Mind* (New York: Weatherhill, 1970).

Tworkov, Helen. *Zen in America* (New York: Kodansha International, 1994).